# Hello
# COLOR

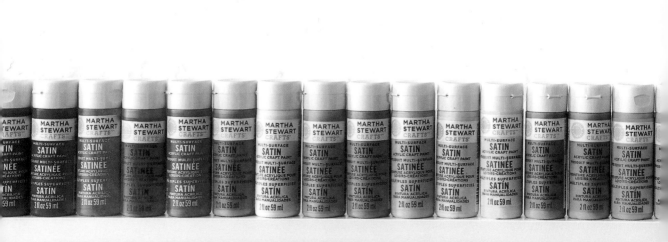

# Hello

# COLOR

## 25 Bright Ideas for DIY Decor

### RACHEL MAE SMITH

## QUIRK BOOKS
### PHILADELPHIA

For my dad—thank you for a lifetime of love,
humor, and always encouraging this birdie to fly.

Library of Congress Cataloging in Publication Number: 2017941581

ISBN: 978-1-68369-017-7

Printed in China
Typeset in Gotham, Lulo, and Sentinel

Designed by Andie Reid

Photographs by Rachel Mae Smith except for the following pages
by Mary Costa: 8, 61 (top left), 95 (top left), 174

Illustration credits: p. 47 by Clare Corfield Carr, pp. 166 and 171 by Jordan Brantley,
p. 167 by Megan Roy, pp. 168 and 169 by Rachael McLean, p. 170 by Christine Herrin,
p. 172 by MJ Kocovski, p. 173 by Sarah Khandjian

Production management by John J. McGurk

Quirk Books
215 Church Street
Philadelphia, PA 19106
quirkbooks.com

10 9 8 7 6 5 4 3 2 1

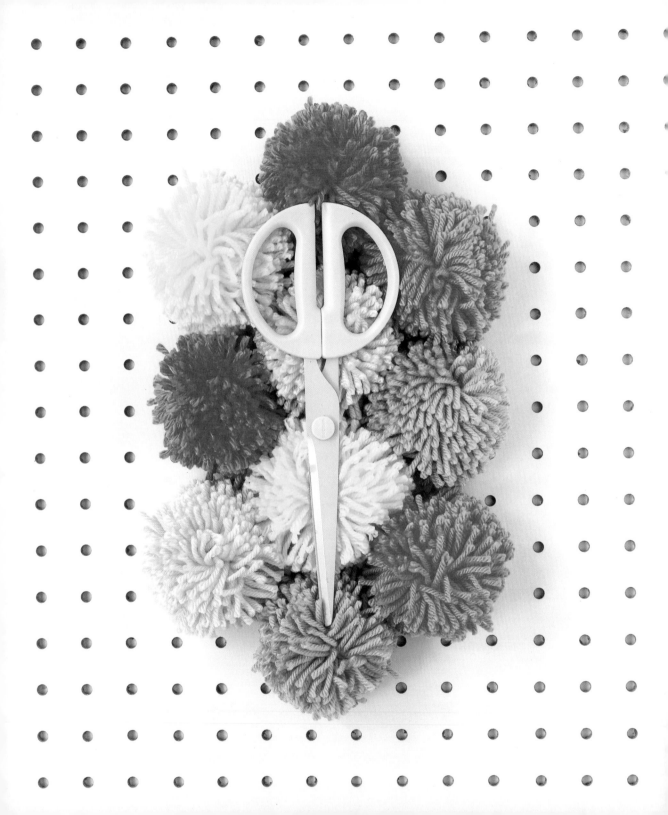

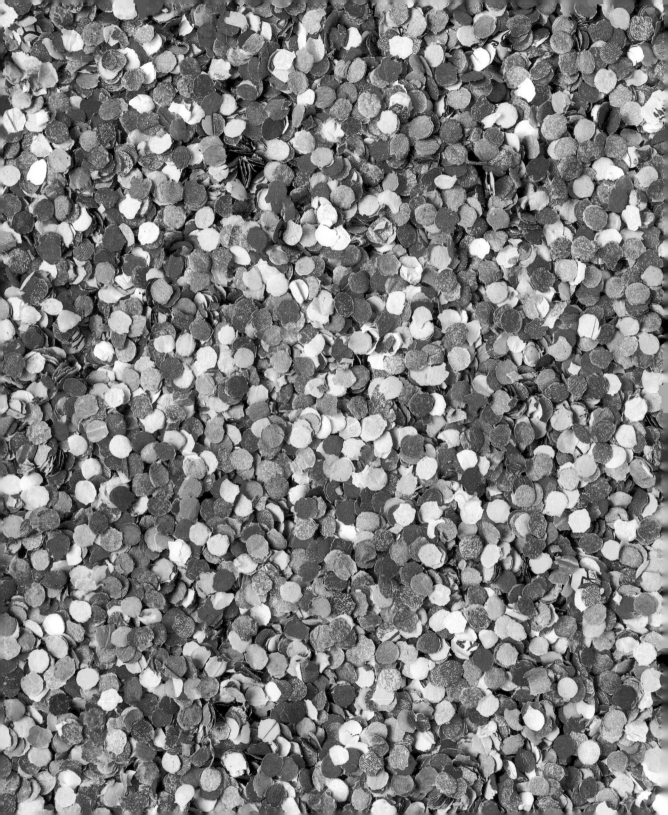

# Contents

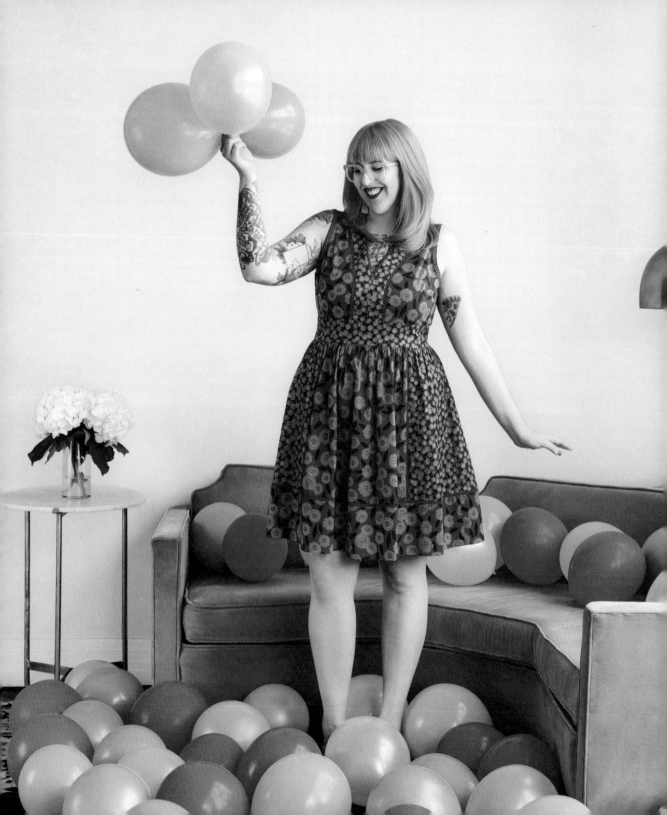

# Welcome to My Colorful World

It's obvious that I *love* color. But it wasn't until I lived in a not-so-colorful place that I discovered just how much. Transitioning from the dreamy pastels of San Francisco to the brick tones of Portland, Oregon, shocked my system. It was this change that made me look closer at the world around me.

To cope with the new scenery, I looked for every bit of brightness I could find. Whether a pop of yellow on a car repair shop, an unexpectedly bold trim on a house, or even just the plants blooming in my neighborhood, I was able to find color almost everywhere I looked. As it turns out, you don't have to live in a colorful place, or have pink hair, to live colorfully—color is always there for those who want to see it.

It's easy to feel timid about adding color to your home—what if it's too bold or you end up hating it? I completely understand! I, too, avoided making the color leap for many years. I thought nothing would match unless everything was neutral, so I didn't take the risk. I worried about spending money on signature pieces only to regret them later. But playing it safe was just no fun! And that's the greatest thing about color: it's *meant* to be fun. You can create your own rules. You can add as much or as little as you wish.

The palettes in *Hello Color* are my personal favorites, but they're only suggestions to help you get started on your own color journey. Think of me as your tour guide. I want you to feel free to explore and experiment with the colors that resonate with you. The ones that make you feel happy, peaceful, or calm. The ones that lift you up and put a smile on your face. The ones that just make you feel *good*.

When it comes to decorating, you don't have to invest a ton of money or time to get the rainbow-hued look you want. In fact, you can make a lot of decorative and artful home-decor items yourself. In this book you'll find fun and easy DIY projects for every room in your home. You'll create artwork that allows you to proudly say "I made it!" when someone asks where it came from, or practical objects that serve a purpose *and* pack a colorful punch. You can even use the tear-out artwork in the back for decor that's easy as can be. But you'll never have to admit that they took less than thirty minutes to do—that's our little secret.

I hope this book inspires you not only to seek color where you live but also to bring your own vision to the space around you. Once you take the leap and start living colorfully, you might wonder how you ever lived before.

xo,

Rachel

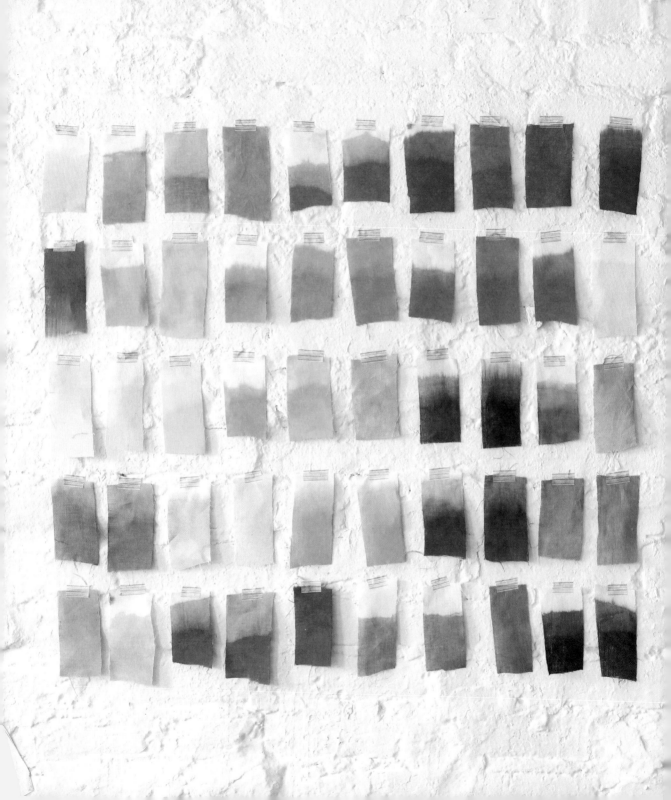

# Color Theory 101

One of the most amazing things about working with color is that it really is subjective. We perceive color based on wavelengths of light that bounce off objects—so, for example, a red apple absorbs all wavelengths but red and reflects those back to our eyes, which then perceive the apple as (you guessed it!) red. But every person's perception is slightly different—and, of course, everyone has different favorites.

Fortunately, colors come in thousands (yes, thousands—Pantone alone has at least 1,114 spot colors) of options. But so many choices can be overwhelming, especially if you're new to decorating, don't know where to start, or just have a hard time making decisions. The good news is that, in all of those thousands of colors, you're bound to find at least one or two bright ones that work in your home. With those selections and a little know-how about mixing and matching, soon you'll be pairing palettes like a pro!

## COLOR TERMS

**PRIMARY COLORS:** The colors that kick off the color wheel—red, blue, and yellow. These hues cannot be formed by any combination of other colors, and all other colors are derived from some mixture of two or three of these bases.

**SECONDARY COLORS:** Colors that result from mixing primary colors together—purple (red + blue), green (blue + yellow), and orange (red + yellow).

**TERTIARY COLORS:** Colors made by mixing adjacent primary and secondary colors. For example, red and orange will give you . . . red-orange!

**TINT:** A lighter version of a base color, created by mixing the color with white.

**SHADE:** A darker version of a base color, created by mixing the color with black.

**VALUE:** The lightness or darkness of a color (i.e., its placement on the spectrum from tint to shade).

**PASTEL:** A soft, delicate, subtle color that reflects a lot of light.

**JEWEL TONE:** A dark, intense color (like a gemstone) that absorbs a lot of light.

**SATURATION:** The intensity of a color, determined by how much the color differs from white; for example, pastels are less saturated than jewel tones.

**TONE:** A less-saturated version of a base color, created by mixing the color with gray.

## BASIC COLOR SCHEMES

In color theory, a *color scheme* is a combination of colors, often drawn from the color wheel. A color scheme forms the basis of your *palette*, or range of colors used in a design. These are the most common combinations.

**COMPLEMENTARY COLORS:** A pair of colors that lie opposite each other on the color wheel. Side by side, they brighten, pop, and have the most contrast of any pairing, but when mixed they become dull and muddy.

**TRIADIC COLOR SCHEME:** A set of colors that are equal distance from one another around the color wheel (typically every fourth color), a slight variation on complementary colors.

**ANALOGOUS COLOR SCHEME:** A set of colors made up of three colors that fall next to one another on the color wheel—for example, red, orange, and yellow.

**MONOCHROMATIC COLOR SCHEME:** A set of colors made up of a base color plus tints and shades of that same color.

Knowing and understanding these words and phrases will help you work with color.

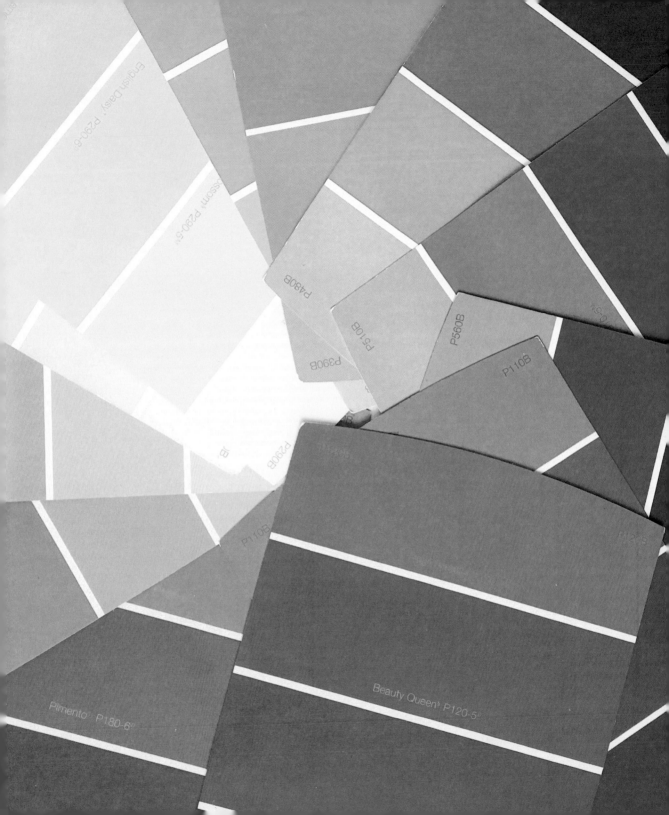

# CREATING A COLOR SCHEME

Rule number one for bringing color into your home: it should make you happy. Home is your own personal space in this world, and above all it should bring you joy. Don't feel as though you have to throw around a bunch of wild colors if you're more of a pastel person, and don't feel bad about breaking the "rules," like no bright colors in the bedroom, only light colors in small spaces, or never put bold colors side by side. If you choose colors you love—from the pieces you buy to the projects you make—I guarantee you'll love the results, too. Simple as that!

For custom-creating your own color scheme, also called a palette, the simplest way to play around with various combinations is to pick up a bunch of paint sample chips from your local hardware store and start laying them out. (And once you've found a combination you like, cut out each of the colors and tape them together on an index card so that your palette is portable.) You can go back and buy the colors of paint you've selected, but you don't *have* to—you can just use the paint chip palette as reference when you buy other supplies and objects. Think of them as color flash cards!

Once you've acquired a bunch of paint chips to play with, it's time to get palette-making. We all know that color preferences are subjective, but there are a few simple tricks that everyone can use to put together a scheme, no matter their individual taste. One good rule of thumb is to select between three and five colors for your palette: one dominant color, plus several supporting and accent colors. This method will help you strike the right balance: if your palette has too few colors, you'll have a harder time distributing your hues because of your limited options. Too many colors and you may find yourself overwhelmed. (Of course if you absolutely must have everything in your house pink, who am I to judge? Just be sure to invite me over for rosé and a selfie!)

For your first color scheme, start with a color you already love and build from there, using one of the classic schemes described on page 12—say, analogous or triadic. Then add and adjust to bring a pop of contrast. For example, if you choose an analogous theme of green and blue, consider adding coral as an accent.

You can also start with a pairing you already love—like pink and yellow, or blue and purple—and see how they look side by side. Then add a shade or tint of one of them, or another color as an accent, to create a palette. (If you don't have a favorite color, work backward from colorful objects or furniture you already own.) Your scheme might not look great at first—maybe two saturated colors like royal purple and mandarin orange compete too much—so try throwing in tints and shades of your colors to create harmony. Combine lighter hues with stronger ones, make an all-pastel palette, or just go all-in and amp up to strong jewel tones—so long as the saturation and value of the jewel tones are close, no one color will look out of place.

Once you've pulled together a starter palette, don't be afraid to tinker! The strongest palettes create a sense of balance and energy: they pull the viewer's eye along without overloading, and they include at least one gentler color (i.e., one with less saturation) for the gaze to "rest" on. If your fave colors feel overwhelming side by side, consider splitting them across multiple palettes

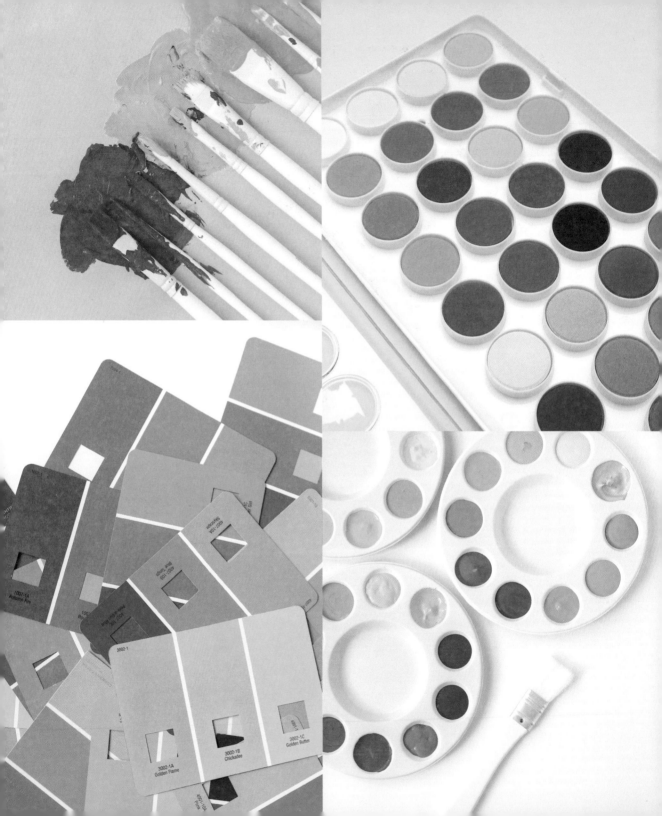

**1** *Start with a scheme
you already love*

and giving each its place to shine. That doesn't mean you have to give up more daring combos, though—although all colors get equal billing on the palette, that arrangement is just an abstract way to see how colors look together. When you go to create décor and set up your space, there's no need to keep even proportions of every color, so you can let one dominate while the others come in with a lighter touch.

After you've mastered the paint chip method, or when you're just looking for more variety, you can step up your schemin' by customizing. Yep, it's time to bust out the paints! Incorporate even more

flexibility by mixing colors yourself. Using acrylic paints and card-stock paper, start dabbing colors together and see what you like. Adjust as you go: mix in white, gray, and black to change the value and saturation of a color, or mix an undertone of one color into another so they harmonize better— for example, dropping some extra blue in green to play off purple. If your scheme is still feeling not quite right, reduce the number of colors—less can be more. Again, there's no wrong way to do it. If you love the colors in your palette and it's not giving you a headache, go for it.

3 *Use decor for inspiration*

4 *Remember that sometimes less can be more!*

Once your palette is optimized, it's time to bring it into the real world. Consider hanging your sample palettes around your home to see how each one matches with your furniture and looks in everyday lighting. Do your purples come off too gloomy in your poorly lit living room? Does the lovely lemon yellow you'd picked for the kitchen feel a little *too* energetic when that early-morning sun hits? Go back, adjust, tweak, and swap. It's just paint and paper, so don't be afraid to strike out beyond your comfort zone. And most of all, have fun!

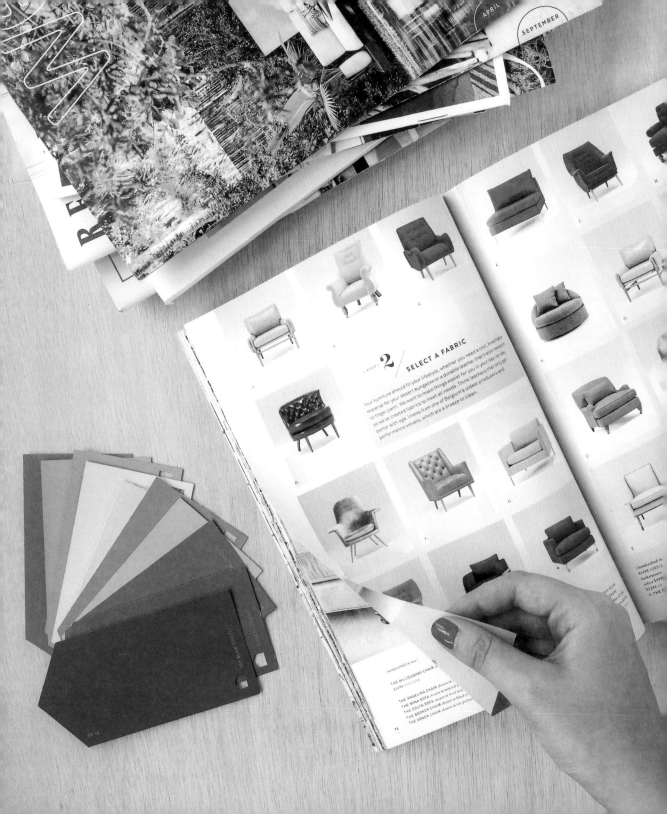

# SHOPPING FOR COLOR

Once you've created a color scheme, it's time to pick up supplies that match your palette. Keep these things in mind before maxing out your credit cards:

**1. START SMALL!** You don't have to buy a bright statement piece of furniture to have a colorful home. There are plenty of other ways to bring your palette into your space. Instead of springing for the new headboard, maybe buy colored sheets (in one of your accent colors). If you want that fun sofa, find a slipcover, reupholster your current couch, or pick up a colorful blanket to spend a little money and seeing whether the color works before fully committing to new furniture.

**2. CHECK THE STORE'S RETURN POLICY BEFORE PURCHASING.** If you can return it, take the item home and see how it looks in your space. For paints or other consumable supplies, ask for sample jars before buying a whole gallon.

**3. GO IN PERSON.** It's so much better to see a color with your own eyes (and not on a screen) before bringing it into your home—plus you'll be less likely to buy multiple shades of the same color since the perfect one will pop out when you view them all together. If possible, look at your fabric/paint/accessory near a window so you can see its "true" color in natural light. If you're trying to match something, bring a fabric swatch (or the clearest phone picture you can manage) with you to the store. Once you feel you have your colors nailed down, note the brand name and color name or number and shop online to your heart's content.

**4. STOCK UP.** Some paints and dyes look very different after one application compared to three. You may need more than you think to achieve the desired saturation (or to repair chips, stains, or fading down the road). Check the package directions, too.

**5. BRING YOUR PALETTE WITH YOU!** If you don't want to tote around a giant painted piece of paper or your paint-chip palette, just snap a (good) picture on your phone for reference.

Of course, the best colorful pieces aren't the ones you find in stores, but the ones you put care into making yourself! Hopefully the projects on the following pages will help you build up color in your home. Do one or all of them. Well, of course, *I* want you to do *all* of them, but if you start with the ones you're drawn to, I think you'll quickly want to try them all. After a bit of practice, you'll be more comfortable and confident coloring your world!

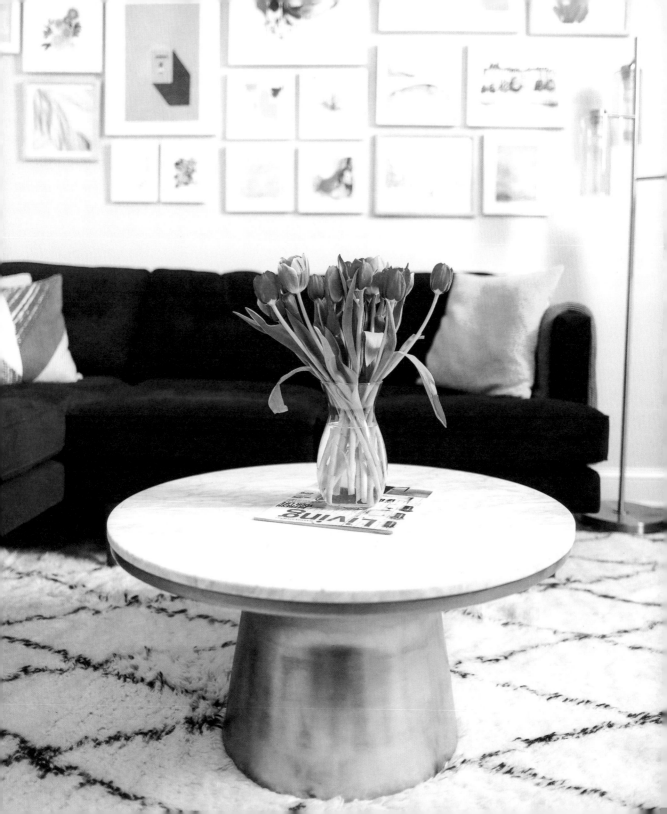

## Chapter One

# THE LIVING ROOM

One of the most highly trafficked areas of the home, the living room should be a warm and welcoming space where you can unwind and entertain. Having handmade elements in this room not only gives your home distinctive visual identity but also becomes a great for topic of discussion when friends and family stop by.

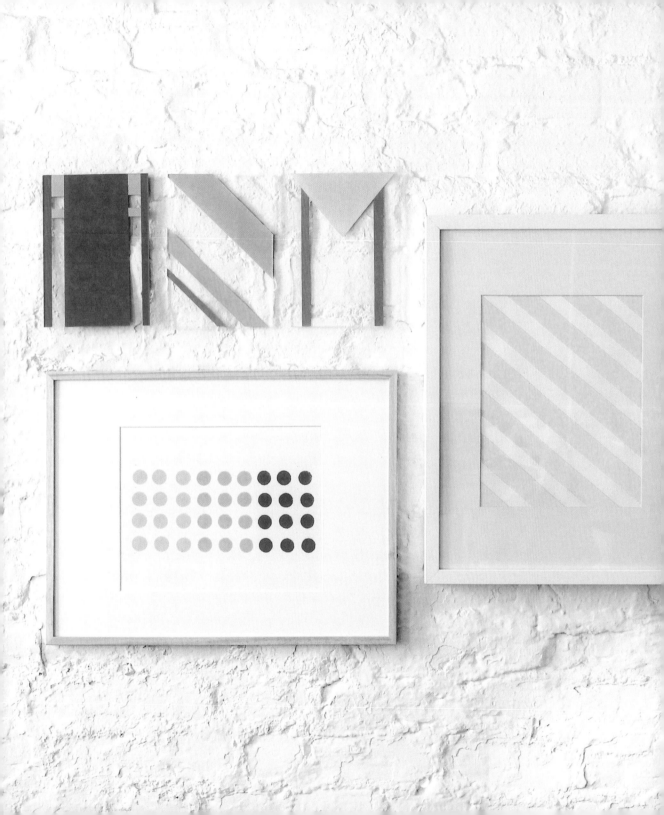

# WALL ART, THREE WAYS

Art doesn't just add instant color and life to your walls—it transforms a whole room! In fact, when you move to a new place, I suggest hanging art as soon as possible to make yourself feel more at home. (Even if you have to move pieces later, it's totally worth it—just use removable adhesive hanging strips instead of nails if you're concerned about damaging the walls.) Whether you keep it minimalistic with a single statement piece or go all-out with a gallery wall, I guarantee your space will feel much more inviting after putting up pieces that make you happy.

Best of all, it's easy to do yourself! Just because professional paintings or sculptures aren't in your budget, or you don't consider yourself an artist, doesn't mean you have to go without. When paired in a repeating pattern, even simple shapes become a work of art! With painted dots, colored paper, and the right palette, your work will look way more upscale than kids' art (even though it's easy enough for a kid to make).

If you're looking to go beyond traditional canvas or paper mediums, try using acrylic sheets. You can fill an entire piece with paint or leave sections blank to work with negative space. Thanks to the transparent material, you needn't be a trained artist to get professional results (hellloooo, tracing!). No matter which option you choose, all you need to make something beautiful for your walls is a bit of skill, a little time, and a few inexpensive supplies.

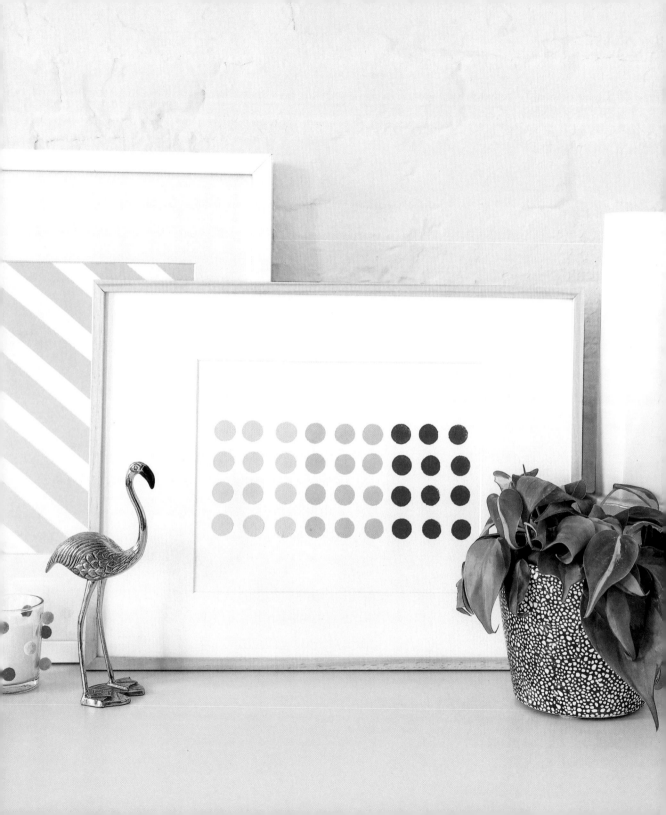

# POLKA DOT ART

1 Cut your paper to fit your frame. Use a pencil to mark the area within the mat (so you know where to paint).

2 Measure and mark guidelines with painter's tape before painting: Decide how many rows of dots you would like, then use the ruler and pencil to measure and mark evenly spaced lines on the paper. Use a strip of painter's tape to connect each set of markings across to create horizontal guidelines. Repeat for the vertical columns.

3 Now it's just a matter of dabbing your pouncer in paint and making dots! Pour paint onto your paper plate or palette and dip your pouncer in, then press the pouncer gently against the paper to make a dot. If you've never worked with a pouncer, make some test dots on scrap paper until you get the hang of it—it should take only a couple tries.

4 Just keep dabbing until your design is complete. Let dry, remove painter's tape, gently erase any visible pencil marks, and then frame to display.

## MATERIALS

Watercolor or BFK paper (available at art supply stores)

Picture frame with mat and glass in your choice of size

X-Acto knife

Cutting mat

Pencil

Ruler

Painter's tape

Acrylic paints

Foam pouncer (available at craft stores and online)

Plastic palette or paper plate

*Making polka dots for this project is especially easy because the foam pouncer is already a circle. (Martha Stewart makes them in a number of sizes.)*

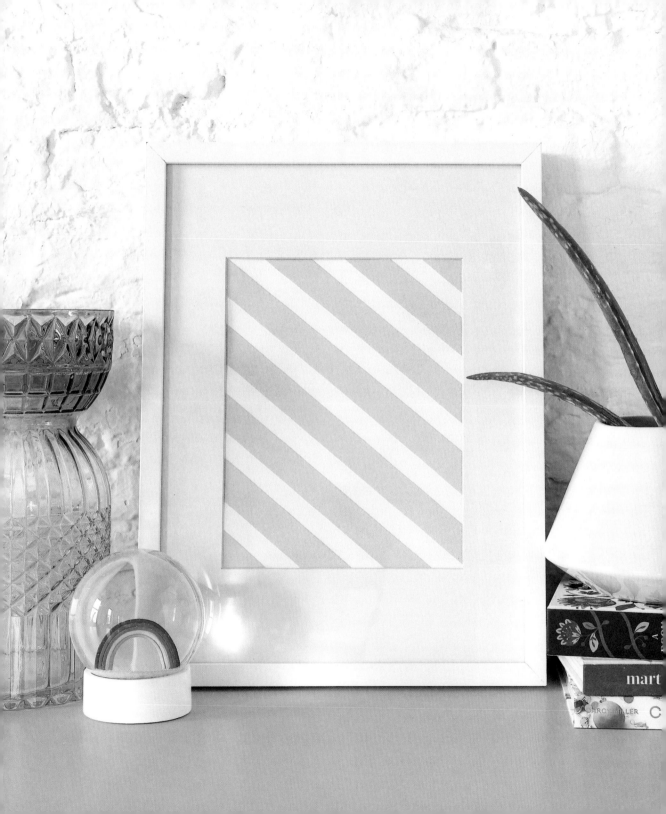

# PAPER CUT-OUT ART

1   Cut the watercolor paper to fit the frame so that the resulting artwork aligns perfectly. It's amazing what a picture frame can do to elevate a project. Even this simple paper collage will look modern and chic.

2   Create some stripes! Stripes are easy to make, and they look great when paired with the painted dots from the previous project. Use scissors to cut your colored paper into strips. Or, if you can't cut a straight line to save your life, try this trick: use an inexpensive ruler, cutting mat, and rotary tool to cut perfectly straight lines. (Keep in mind that a rotary tool is dangerously sharp, and you should always protect your hands when using one.)

3   Once you've cut your strips, arrange them on the watercolor paper in a pattern you like. Use the foam brush to apply a thin layer of Mod Podge on the back of each strip and glue in place. Let dry completely. Then frame, hang, and enjoy.

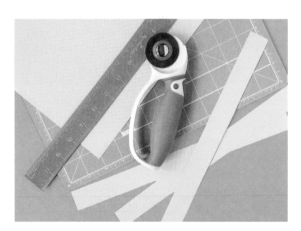

## MATERIALS

Watercolor paper

Colored/patterned paper

Scissors

Rotary tool, cutting mat, and ruler (optional)

Mod Podge

Foam brush

Picture frame with mat and glass in your choice of size

> *You can use any paper for your base, but thicker art papers (instead of printer sheets) have a nice texture and color. Also experiment with patterned scrap-booking paper or fancy wrapping paper sold by the sheet.*

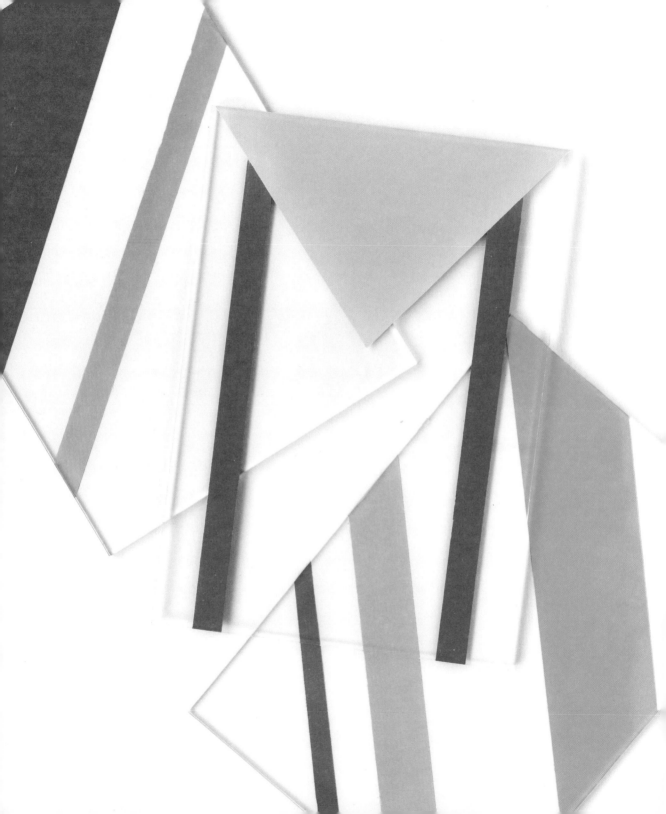

# ACRYLIC ART

1 If you'd like to eventually hang your artwork, use the power drill to make holes in the acrylic sheet for the mounting hardware before you start painting.

2 Plan your design. Use the tape to mark where you'd like to paint. If incorporating letters or numbers into your design, keep in mind they will appear backward when you flip over the acrylic sheet to display because the side of acrylic that you're painting will end up being the back of the art, closest to the wall. Also, if you plan to mount your piece on a wall (instead of propping it on a shelf or vanity), consider where you'll attach the hanger or picture-hanging strips—you may want to use a darker color or a more solid line in that place so that it doesn't show through the front.

3 Paint! To keep things very simple (mainly because my painting skills aren't the strongest), I used washi tape in different widths and paint to create simple geometric patterns. Because the acrylic sheet is clear, you can easily trace any design you want. Again, remember to reverse the image so that it will appear the correct way once flipped over.

4 Let the paint dry, then display your artwork. You can use removable hanging strips or hook-and-loop fasteners on the back if you want the piece to hang seamlessly, or nails and mounting brackets if you drilled holes.

MATERIALS

Clear acrylic sheet, $\frac{1}{8}$" thick

Power drill, picture-hanging nails, and mounting brackets (optional)

Acrylic paint

Paintbrush

Paper plate or palette

Painter's tape or washi tape

Removable picture-hanging strips or hook-and-loop fasteners (optional)

*I was able to find Plexiglas on the internet, but acrylic sheets are sold at hardware stores, too. There are many sizes to choose from (you can even get it cut in a circle!), so start small to see if you like working with this material before investing in a larger size.*

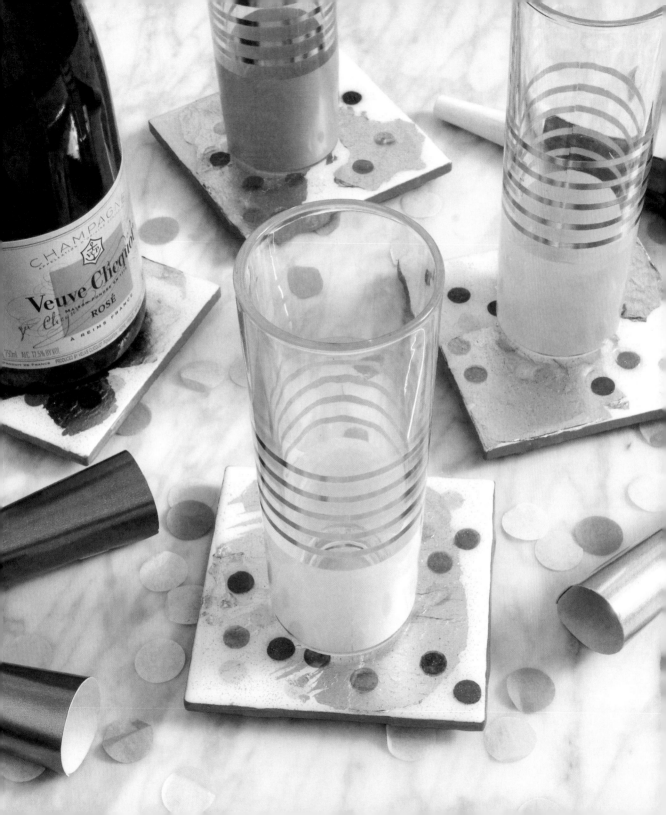

# PARTY ANIMAL COASTERS

## MATERIALS

Foam poster board

Ceramic bathroom tiles

Acrylic paint and brush (optional)

Wooden block, slightly smaller than the tiles

Gold leaf and glitter (optional)

Colorful confetti

Clear casting epoxy resin (see tips on page 34)

Craft sticks

Plastic cups

Gloves

Drinking straw

Small self-stick foam circles

You may be a party animal at heart, but deep down you know you don't want any water rings (or, okay, wineglass stains) on the top of your nice coffee table. Don't worry! Let everyone know you're still the life of the party by handing out these cute confetti coasters.

*The key to this project is picking the right confetti. All confetti is wonderful for throwing in the air, but some kinds work better when mixed with epoxy. Use a flat type (round tissue-paper confetti instead of zigzag packing confetti) so that it hardens smooth on the tile. Or try making your own. All you need are tissue paper and scissors. Cut the paper into strips and then into smaller squares/triangles. Fringe scissors speed up the process.*

1    Prep your work station. Choose a well-ventilated area and cover your work surface in case of spills or drips. Lay the poster board on top of the covered, flat surface (this is the key to making sure your coasters dry evenly).

2    For an extra pop of color, you can paint the tile edges with bright acrylic paint if you'd like. Tape off the tops of the tiles to avoid getting paint on the surface (unless your tiles are glazed, in which case any excess paint should wipe right off) and paint. Let dry before continuing.

3    Place the tiles in the center of the wooden block. When you pour the epoxy over the tile in step 6, the block will allow excess liquid to drip off the sides and onto the poster board, leaving your coasters with smooth edges.

4    Apply gold leaf to your tiles, if desired: brush water onto the tile, leaving some patches dry, then press leaf sheet on top. Any leaf not stuck to the water should flake off, creating a loose, organic look. Alternatively, you can tear the leaf sheet into pieces, then brush the tile with water and press torn pieces in place. (Gold leaf may come with special adhesive, but there's no need for it in this project since the epoxy will seal the leaf in place.)

5    Arrange confetti on your tiles. The confetti will move slightly when the epoxy is poured, so leave space around the tile edges to keep the pieces from running off. For more shimmer and flair, add a sprinkle of glitter! Make sure everything is lying flat (avoid layering confetti) so that the epoxy dries smooth.

6  Put on gloves for this step! In a plastic cup, use the craft sticks to mix epoxy according to the manufacturer's instructions. Most call for a 1:1 ratio and a double-pour mixture, but it's best to follow the exact instructions. (See tips on page 34.) Pour mixture over tiles. A little goes a long way and you have plenty of time to work, so don't rush and coat the entire surface immediately. Excess epoxy will drip off the tiles and form bumps (and it will harden this way). If you notice that happening, wipe off excess from the tile edges while wearing gloves.

7  Once your coaster is completely covered and has settled a bit, pop air bubbles on the surface by blowing on them through a straw. (Caution: Epoxy is a harsh chemical, so *do not inhale* during this step!) It will be obvious when the epoxy starts to harden. Set tiles aside for 24 hours to harden completely.

8  Apply the self-adhesive foam circles to the tile bottoms, one on each corner. Now your coasters are ready for a glass of water (or wine)!

# TIPS FOR WORKING WITH EPOXY RESIN

*Wear gloves*

From home decor pieces to jewelry to trinkets galore, you can create just about anything with epoxy resin, even as a beginner! (There are many types of resin, but epoxy resin is easiest to work with and the best choice for beginners.) If you've never worked with epoxy, here are a few simple tips to ensure the best results for you and whatever you're making.

*Stick to the instructions*

+ Always work in a well-ventilated space and wear gloves. Fumes from epoxy resin can be harmful, so please take safety precautions! Plus, it can be really sticky and hard to remove if you come into contact with it, and who wants that hassle?

+ Follow manufacturer instructions—but like, *really* follow them. Stick to the set ratios and do the double pour as directed. I know you think you'll save time if you skip it, but do it anyway. If the resin isn't mixed properly, it may not set correctly and you'll have to redo the entire project, which isn't saving time at all. You'll have about 15–20 minutes to work before the resin hardens, so there's no need to rush.

*Stir slowly*

+ When mixing the hardener and resin, stir slowly, keeping the stir stick at the bottom of the cup. The faster you stir and the more you lift the stick, the more air bubbles you'll whip into your mix. Air bubbles will harden in the resin, and your piece will not come out as clearly or as smooth as you want it to.

+ You can remove air bubbles by blowing on them through a straw. It's important *not* to inhale the fumes during this process! You can also try a heat gun, but use for a limited time to avoid damaging your mold.

*Remove bubbles with a straw*

+ If you need to smooth the edges of your final resin object, fill a container with water and sandpaper it underwater. This method will keep you from breathing in the dust that comes off when sanding.

# CATCH-ALL MINI TRAY

## MATERIALS

Small wooden tray

Cardboard or newspaper

Spray paint in varying shades

Clear acrylic sealant

Stickers

Ruler

Between kicking off our shoes and changing into sweatpants after a long day, we can—and often do—lose our keys in the post-work shuffle. To save you hours of searching, create a dedicated place in your home where, when you walk in the door, you can set down everything you're carrying (keys, phone, wallet). To wrangle it all in one place, and to help you establish a routine so you can find things easily, make yourself a catch-all tray in a bright eye-catching color scheme! Because no one has time to ask their loved ones (or their pets) "Have you seen my keys?" every time they leave the house!

*For this project I used a plaque from the wood hobby section of the craft store, but you could use just about any tray or dish you like. I recommend one with a raised edge that will keep loose items in place.*

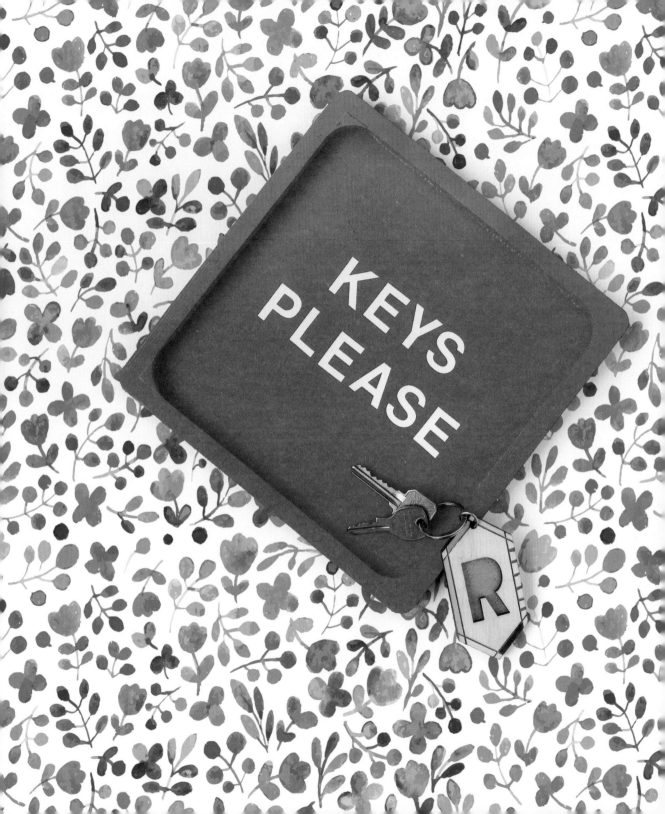

1. Working in a well-ventilated area, lay out cardboard or newspaper to protect your work surface. Spray-paint your tray. For a gradient look, paint the entire piece one color, then spray with a lighter hue in one corner and a darker hue in the opposite corner (dividing the tray into thirds). Let dry.

2. Seal with a coat of clear acrylic and let dry.

3. Arrange your stickers. It helps to use a ruler to align everything evenly (particularly if you're using letters to spell something out). You may also want to place them lightly at first—meaning not fully stuck on, in case you need to reposition them. Once you've settled on the placement, run your fingernail over the letters to secure them.

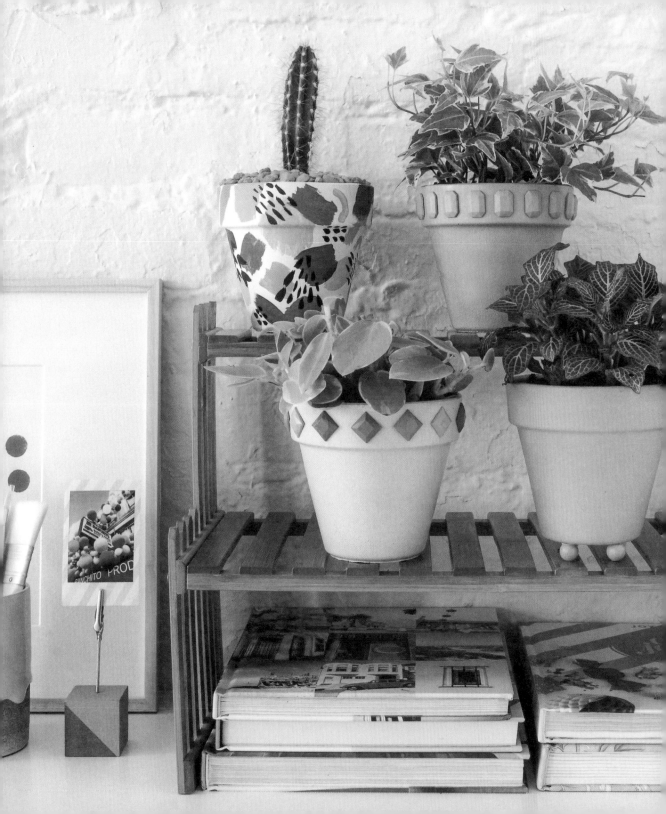

# COLORFUL PLANTER,
## THREE WAYS

There are few things in this world I love more than rhinestones (okay, that may be a bit of an exaggeration, but my love for all things sparkly is very real). Though I'm happy wearing rhinestones in my day-to-day outfits, I also found the perfect way to bring them into my home decor as well: putting them on a planter!

Even if rhinestones aren't your thing, you can do better than that boring plastic pot most plants come in. You don't have to be a professional painter to make a lovely abstract planter—in fact, all you really need to be able to do is hold a brush and paint a few basic shapes. The nice thing about working abstractly is that there's no right or wrong way to do it. So get ready to brag about how great an artist you are—it can be our little secret that it was actually very simple. Finally, adding little wooden feet is a great way to make a pot stand out—literally!

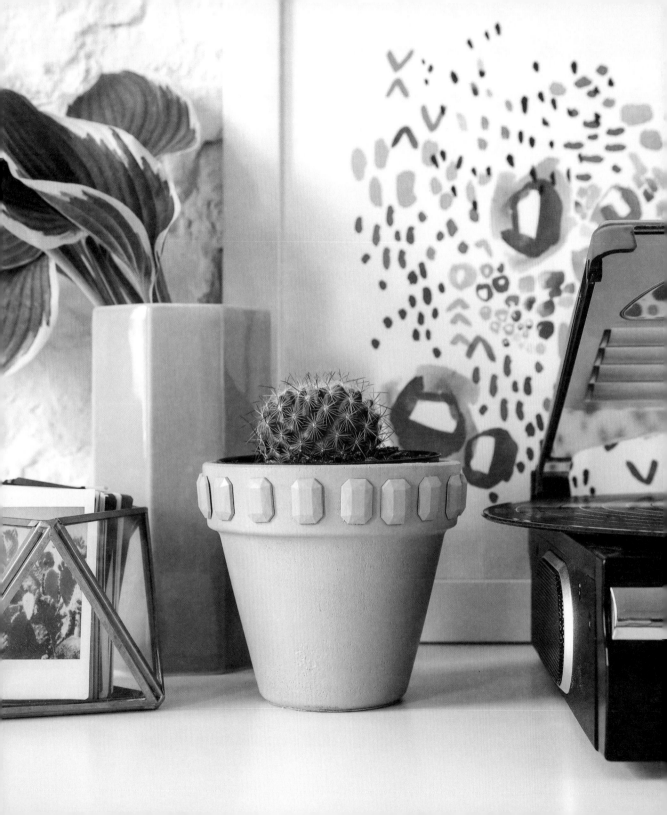

# BEJEWELED PLANTER

1 Working in a well-ventilated area and on a covered surface, spray-paint your planter the color of your choice and let dry.

2 Glue the rhinestones to the planter in the design of your choice. Here are three to try:

TEXTURED: The easiest way to add dimension to your planter. Glue on rhinestones, let dry, and then spray-paint the entire surface. You can create just about any pattern with the stones and the results will look great.

AROUND THE RIM: Simple and sweet. Depending on the plant, you may see only a bit of the rhinestones peeking out. This is definitely the safest bet if you're a little nervous about adding flair to your home decor.

SHAPES: Cover the entire planter in shapes, or keep it simple with a single statement shape. First, spray-paint the planter; then, with a pencil, lightly draw your shape. Fill it with rhinestones and let the glue dry. Erase any visible pencil marks.

3 Use the potting soil to pot your plant in its sparkly new planter. Ta-da!

## MATERIALS

Terra-cotta planter

Spray paint

Clear acrylic sealant (optional)

Assorted rhinestones

E-6000 glue

Plant (see page 46)

Potting soil

*You can totally invest in fancy rhinestones—I'd never stop you!—but if you're looking for something more cost efficient, buy the cheap plastic ones from the craft store (yep, the "jewels" that look a little cheesy) and hit them with some spray paint. They'll lose a bit of their shine but you'll be left with fun textured stones that look nicely sophisticated. If you want to keep some sheen, coat them with gloss spray paint instead of matte. Seal with clear acrylic spray to avoid chipping when gluing them on.*

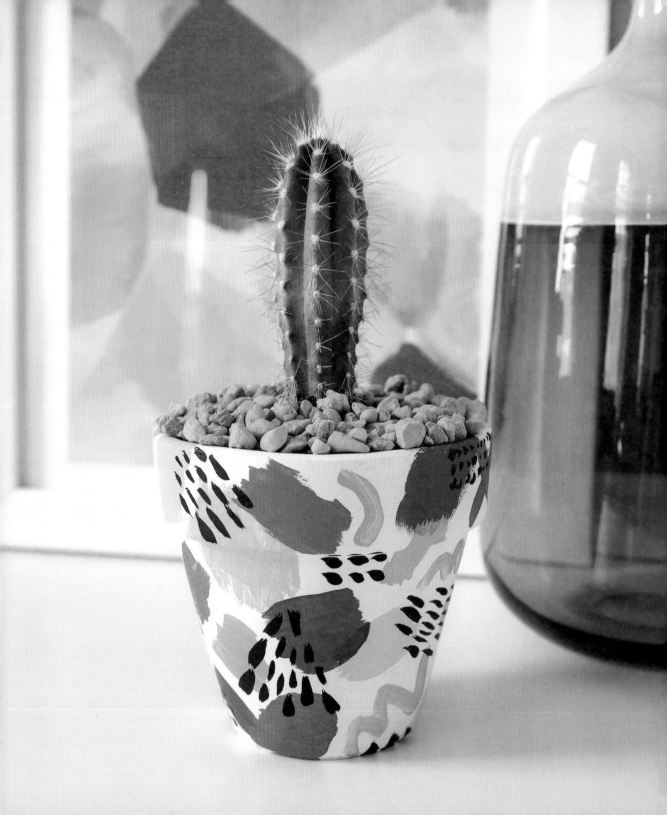

# ABSTRACT PAINTED PLANTER

1 Paint your planter one solid base color. For a smooth, even coat, spray paint works best, but you can also use acrylic paint and a brush. White is perfect if you plan to use a lot of colors throughout (you won't have to worry about clashing). Be sure to paint over the rim and a few inches inside the planter so that some color peeks out after your plant is potted. Also, when you don't limit yourself to painting just below the exterior rim, you can go even bolder with your design!

2 Once the base color is dry, it's time to create your design. If you're nervous about working freehand, use a pencil to lightly draw the shape/location of your patterns. Think of the planter as an oddly shaped canvas.

3 Get painting! It helps to have all the colors poured out on your palette or paper plate, with a brush for each color. If you plan to overlap colors, let each color dry before you paint over it with another so that you don't muddy them. Consider adding a small pattern detail, like a cluster of dots or dashes, for variety. Keep painting and creating shapes until your planter is covered or until you're happy, whichever comes first!

4 Spray the planter with acrylic sealant, let dry, and then pot your plant.

Terra-cotta planter

Spray paint

Acrylic paints

Paintbrushes in varying sizes

Paper plate or paint palette

Pencil

Clear acrylic sealant

Plant (see page 46)

Potting soil

*I've found that paint easily chips off plastic planters, so to keep your hard work intact, opt for terra-cotta. The porous surface will absorb the paint, making it less likely to flake off. It also helps seal your planter to extend its life.*

EMILY
HENDERSON  STYLED

LIVING WITH PATTERN  REBECCA ATWOOD  POTTER

# FOOTED PLANTER

1 Turn your planter upside down and arrange the wooden beads where you'd like the "feet" of the planter. Play around, testing different approaches with the beads before gluing down—you'll want to place them on the edges, with equal space between them. I used 4 total to create equal balance, but you could try a different way. For example, you could use 5 to 8 beads, depending on the size, and arrange them side by side in a ring around the bottom. When you're satisfied with placement, affix the beads to the bottom of the planter with the glue. Let dry.

2 When glue is dry, turn planter right side up, and spray paint the entire thing. Small quick strokes will help you create a nice even application without drips or bubbles. (I also recommend applying two coats for the best coverage.) Let the paint dry completely.

3 Fill with your favorite plant and the potting soil and you're all done!

## MATERIALS

Planter

4–8 wooden beads

E-6000 glue

Spray paint

Plant (see page 46)

Potting soil

*This DIY raised planter adds a little bit of unexpected height to a traditional pot. Painting the planter one color overall will make it look sleek, like it was manu-factured that way. But! If you want an extra kick of color, paint the beads a dif-ferent color from the planter before attaching them..*

# FIVE HARD-TO-KILL HOUSEPLANTS

Houseplants are the easiest way to add warmth and life to any room. Not only do they help clean the air, but they also make just about any space feel instantly calm. (Seriously, whenever you're in doubt about how to fill a blank space, add a plant and thank me later.) And every new plant needs a nice new planter, which is an easy way to sneak a colorful DIY into your decor!

But if plants tend not to thrive under your care, you might be hesitant to make the investment. And rightly so! They're not always cheap, and it's such a bummer when they die. (The number of plants I've accidentally killed over the years is well into the double digits, so I completely understand.) The good news is that there's hope for those of us who lack a green thumb. These five hardy houseplants can survive occasional periods of neglect, and they look great to boot.

*Check labels for water and sun schedules when placing plants in your house. If you'd like other types of plants in your home than those listed here, visit a greenhouse and talk to the staff gardener about plants that have similar watering needs. Have one watering day for all instead of having to keep track of multiple schedules will help reduce the risk of killing your plants.*

+ **SANSEVIERIA** (aka snake plant or mother-in-law's tongue): Don't let the common names fool you! This plant, with its bold, bladelike leaves, is extremely easy to care for and can be left to its own devices for weeks at a time.

+ **CHLOROPHYTUM COMOSUM** (aka spider plant): Easy to grow and maintain, it even produces little flowers if given enough daylight!

+ **ALOE VERA:** This spiky succulent is great for displaying in a sunny kitchen window, and it's wonderful to have on hand in case of burns.

+ **ASPIDISTRA ELATIOR** (aka cast iron plant): As the common name suggests, this is one tough plant. It'll do just fine even if it doesn't get a lot of light.

+ **POTHOS** (aka devil's ivy): This pretty vine has lovely variegated leaves and looks superb in a hanging basket.

A WORD OF CAUTION: Although these plants look great in any home, they are not necessarily pet friendly. Please check with your vet before purchasing!

Chlorophytum comosum

Aspidistra elatior

Sansevieria

Aloe vera

Pothos

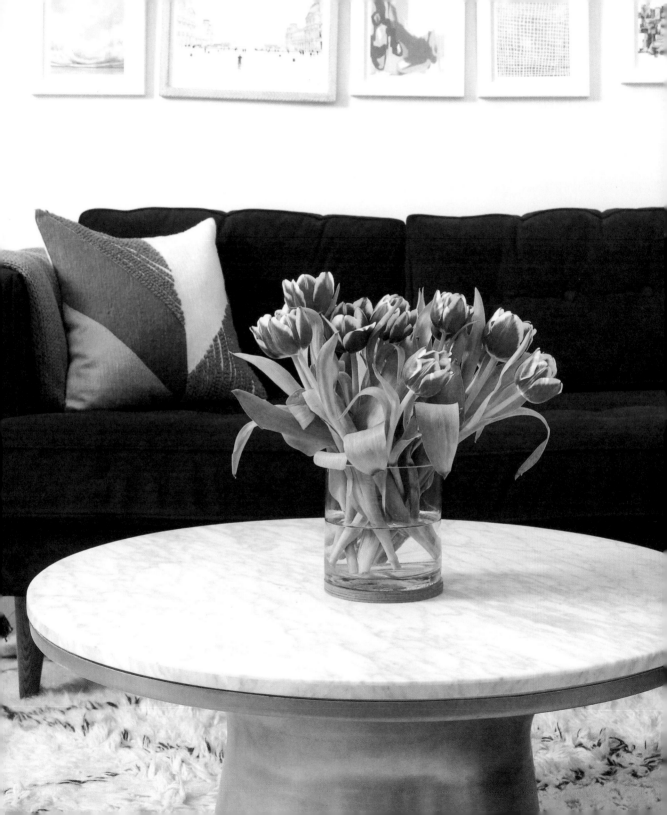

# FANCY FOOTED VASE

Wood rounds (available at craft stores or online)

Wood glue and clamps (if gluing rounds together)

Acrylic paint

Paintbrushes

Paper plate or paint palette

Clear shellac

E-6000 glue

Glass vase

If you want to make your vases unique without using traditional glass paint, try adding a colorful base instead. It adds unexpected height and another texture, creating more visual variety. Plus, the woodgrain and flowers are a match made in heaven!

*You can choose a vase and wood round of any size, but they should have the same diameter. For this project, I chose a 5-inch vase and 5-inch wood rounds.*

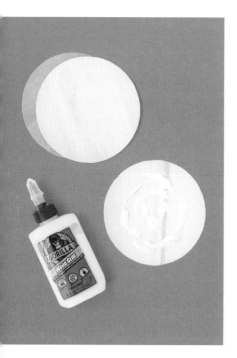

1   If you can't find a thick wood round, glue together multiple thinner rounds (which is what I did here): Apply wood glue to one round and lay it on top of a second round. Repeat as necessary to desired thickness, then use the clamp to hold the rounds in place. Wipe glue from the sides with a damp cloth. Let dry.

2   Paint time! Use the paintbrush to cover the wood round with your color of choice, then let dry. Because the bottom of your vase is clear, the color on the top round will reflect a little through the water. Once the round is dry, seal with clear shellac.

3   Apply a thin ring of E-6000 glue around the top edge of your wood round and affix your vase to it. Allow to dry upright, with the wood on bottom and vase on top. You may need to hold it in place for 2–3 minutes to ensure that the round and vase dry directly on top of each other.

4   When the glue is completely dry, fill your vase with flowers and enjoy! To maintain the quality of the vase, spot-clean with a damp cloth and avoid submerging in water.

# POM-POM
# BASKET

MATERIALS

Yarn in various colors

Pom-pom maker (available at craft stores or online)

Scissors

Pin backs or safety pins

Woven basket

The last thing anyone wants to do mid-movie is get up and search for a blanket in the dark. For easy-access storage without compromising on closet space or good looks, cover a blanket basket with playful homemade pom-poms. It will help keep your space tidy and allow you to quickly tuck away those throws at a moment's notice. Unexpected guests will never know you just spent the past six hours napping on the couch.

*Attaching the pom-poms with pins provides flexibility that hot glue just does not. You can change the color scheme for a fresh look (or to match a new piece of decor), replace damaged poms (instead of hiding the wonky section against the wall), upgrade to a new basket, or just start from scratch and do something completely different!*

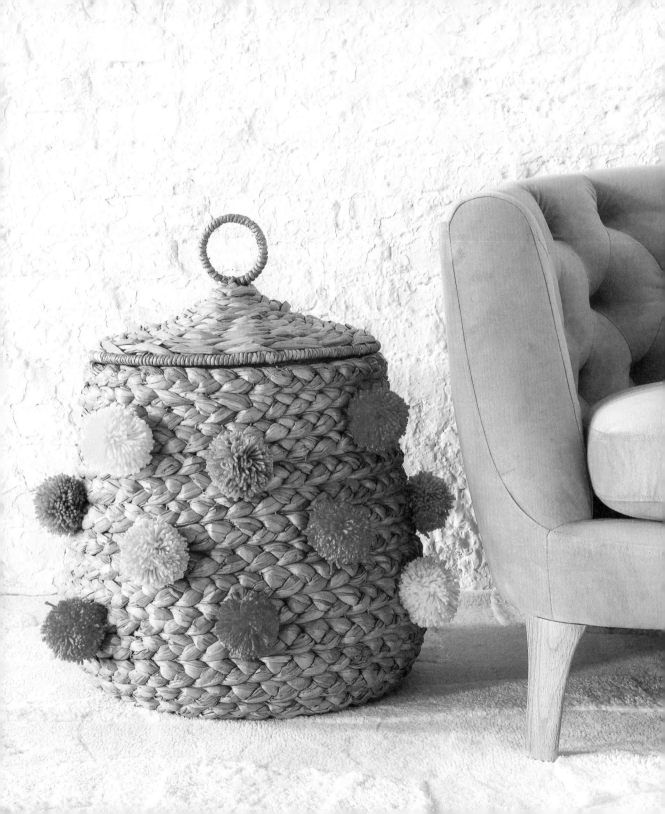

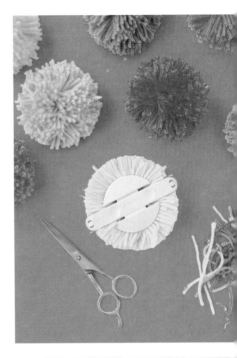

1. It's time to learn how to make a pom-pom! With a plastic pom-pom maker (yup, that really is the name of the tool), you'll be able to crank out a batch in no time at all. Although you can make poms without it, this specialized tool is great for getting them all roughly the same size. If you want variety, pick up a few makers in different sizes.

   Open the arms of your pom-pom maker, starting with the two tabs that face the same direction. Wrap yarn around both the arms (don't wrap the arms individually; wrap them together) until they're completely covered, then close. Repeat on the other side. The more yarn you add, the fluffier your pom-pom will be.

2. Using sharp scissors, snip the yarn along the center path of the tool until you've gone all the way around.

3. Cut a separate length of yarn. Slip it through the center path and knot it around the middle of the tool to secure the pom.

4. Remove yarn from the tool, trim the ends to make them even, and fluff out the pom. Then repeat, repeat, repeat until you've got all the poms you want.

5. Once you finish making pom-poms, it's time to pin them in place. Holding a pom, loop one arm of a pin back around the pom's center loop, then fasten the pin on the basket. Repeat until the basket is covered to your liking. Fill your pom-pommed basket with throws and enjoy!

# BASKET CASE

Baskets come in so many varieties that even if you and your BFF do this project together, you'll still end up with completely different results. The basket material you choose is up to you; just make sure you can pierce it with a pin to attach your pom-poms! Here are a few suggestions:

**+ SEAGRASS BASKET:** A woven basket made of this natural and easily braided material.

**+ BELLY BASKET:** Also typically woven from seagrass; folds up and stores easily.

**+ ROPE BASKET:** Made from sewn cotton rope; comes in a variety of colors, including white. The white can be dyed to work with your color palette.

*Belly basket*

*Rope basket*

*Seagrass basket*

# Bar Carts for Beginners

Whether you're serving cocktails or mocktails, a bar cart is the perfect way to bring a social element to any room. Before you can knock your guests' socks off with your mixology skills, the first thing they'll see is your great styling. You want to create a space where you can welcome people and offer them a drink—it doesn't have to be traditional or expected.

First things first: the cart. You can buy a dedicated piece of furniture, but you don't need one to have a home bar. Try reserving a small section atop an entertainment center (I recommend displaying bottles on a nice tray if you take this route), or mounting shelves on the wall. (Open shelving can be tricky because you can't hide the clutter, but there are a few easy tips that are sure to help you impress.) Bar carts come in tons of styles, from romantic to sleek to midcentury modern and beyond, so if you have the space (and funds) for one, you'll surely find a style that fits seamlessly with your decor.

Once you have selected and cleared off your space, it's time to stock it! Here's how.

## DRINKS

Because, really, what's a bar without booze?! Wine and beer are staples, and I highly recommend having them both on hand (meaning, in the fridge), but your cart is all about fun cocktails. To be able to make a variety of drinks, grab one bottle of each basic liquor:

| | |
|---|---|
| RUM | VODKA |
| WHISKEY | TEQUILA |
| GIN | |

You don't have to spring for top-shelf spirits; start with small bottles, and build up to nicer brands once you find the ones you like. For a safe bet, local distilleries will likely have the cutest packaging, plus you'll be supporting businesses in your community. You can wait to buy specialty drink ingredients like bitters and simple syrups until you know which recipes you plan to make.

As far as mixers go, seltzer and tonic water are must-haves; they're great for both cocktails and mocktails and will be used time and again. Sparkling juices and specialty mixers will also help you create a delicious drink for designated drivers and friends who do not consume alcohol. To be a top-notch host, and to channel your inner Martha, think of what your friends and family members like to drink as well as your own tastes when stocking supplies, even if that means picking up bottles you wouldn't ordinarily buy.

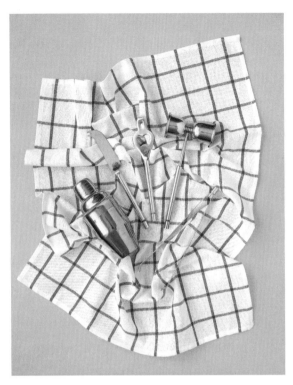

## TOOLS

Some cocktails require more effort than pouring liquid over ice, so stock your bar with the tools of the trade. You can typically buy these items in sets to eliminate the guesswork, or you can build your own kit piece by piece. Here's what you'll need to conquer making any drink in style:

| | |
|---|---|
| SHAKER | STRAINER |
| JIGGER | JUICER |
| ICE BUCKET | MUDDLER |
| BOTTLE OPENER | CORKSCREW |

## GLASSWARE

Here's where you can be playful and throw rules out the window. Since you won't use these glasses daily, try something special, like a funky pattern or bright color. Vintage and antiques stores will have gorgeous pieces, though they might be a bit pricey. Take your time investing and building your collection. And remember to store glasses with the opening facedown so they don't collect dust.

# PUTTING IT ALL TOGETHER

To send your styling over the top, attend to the details of your bar cart, even when it comes to the basics. For example, patterned straws in a cute container are not only functional and organized but also fun and unexpected. Consider these styling tips as you finalize your drinks station:

- If you're new to making drinks, **PICK UP A FEW COCKTAIL BOOKS**. Try to get one with the basics and one with more adventurous concoctions. Not only will these help you learn a new skill, but you'll also have pretty covers to display by your cart.

- **CLUSTERING BOTTLES** near a serving tray or marble slab makes for a practical and pretty presentation.

- Setting out a **GROUP OF SIMILAR, NON-BOOZE BOTTLES** (like seltzer water) creates order and flow. Plus, it's a cheaper way to fill space than with additional liquor.

- If your favorite liquor has an ugly label, **DISPLAY IT IN A DECANTER**. To add a pop of fun, DIY yourself some drink tags!

- To soften the look, **ADD A VASE** with faux or real flowers. You can buy gorgeous silk flowers or preserved eucalyptus (my go-to), which not only smells great but also lasts much longer than a fresh bouquet.

- Place or prop **ART ABOVE OR ON YOUR CART**. Try the projects on page 23 for an additional conversation starter.

- For garnish and even more color, **KEEP A BOWL OF FRUIT NEARBY**. Oranges, lemons, and limes are often called for in drinks. If you don't entertain frequently, display faux lemons for the same citrusy twist of color.

Above all, remember that you don't have to be a bartender to have a well-stocked and functional bar cart. Have fun! Learn what you like, the recipes your guests enjoy, and the drinks your guests request, and go from there. Cheers!

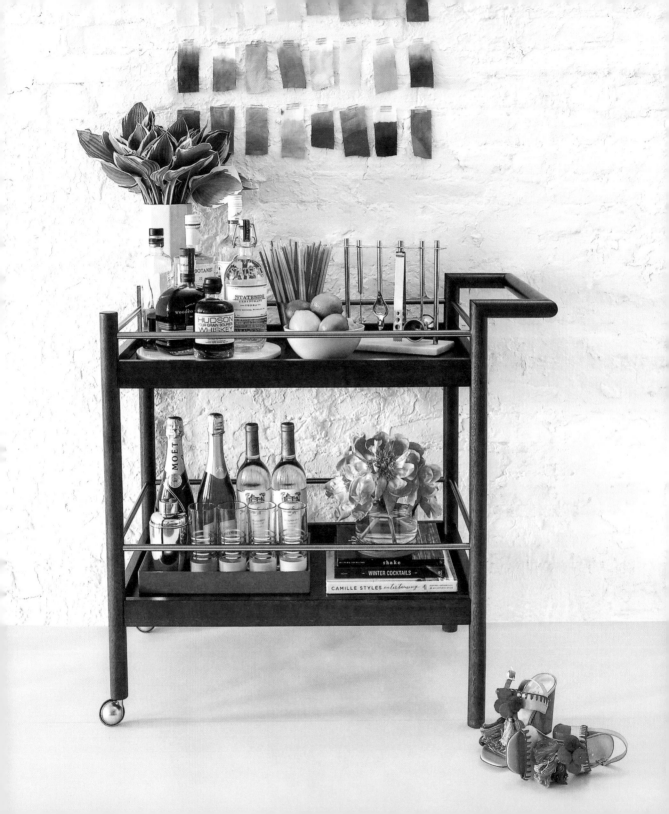

# Amp Up Your Neutrals

If you're new to adding color into your home and want to dip your toe in the rainbow pool, the best place to start is by playing with neutrals. Neutral colors tend to be a safe bet, especially when purchasing larger furniture pieces, because you can mix and match them with different colors throughout the seasons and over the years. Then you can weave in color until you feel more comfortable pulling the trigger on that vibrant sofa you *really* want but aren't sure you can pull off. (You can totally pull it off. But we'll work up to that!)

Want to pair neutrals with something unexpected? These foolproof pairings can help you step up your color game.

## GRAY

Gray is a softer neutral that pairs nicely with school-bus yellow, coral, and green. A lighter gray will help make colors pop while taking wear and tear (and spills!) better than white.

## BROWN

Many furniture pieces have wooden elements in a shade of brown, so you'll probably end up having to match it at some point. When picking browns, opt for wood with warmer undertones, then pair it with a deeper blue, chartreuse, or rich pink.

## WHITE

Really, what color *doesn't* look good with white? For a bold look, pair it with brights like aqua, red plum, and orange, instead of softer pastels. A white rug can brighten a space and make it feel larger, thanks to its light-reflecting qualities.

## NAVY

This dark blue is perfect if you want to shy away from black—it's still a deep, rich color, but it reads a little less harsh. Pair with brighter colors and shades of pink, yellow, and teal to help the deep hue pop.

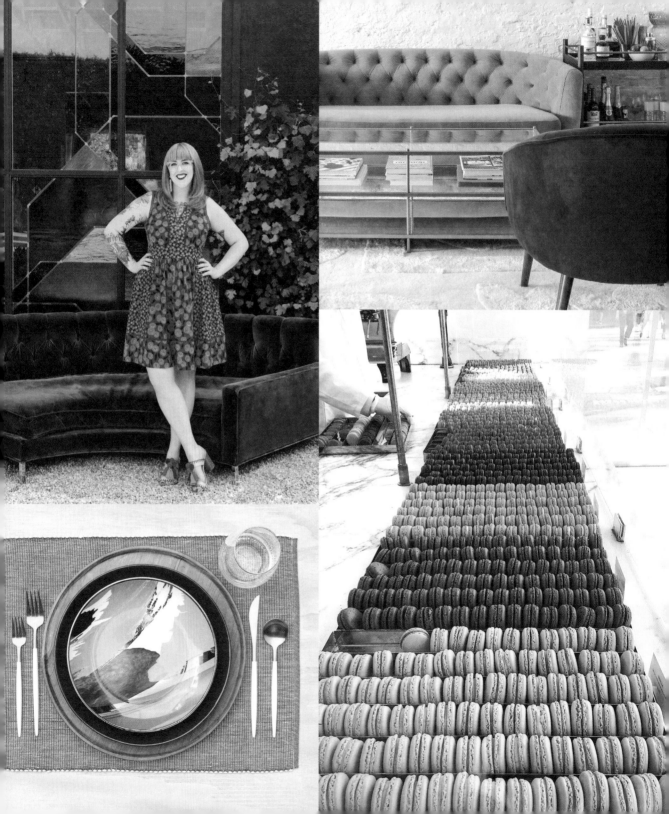

## HOW TO APPLY

If you're building slowly on neutrals, start with accessories and other pieces that are easy to swap out. Pillows are a quick and easy way to make over a couch without changing everything. Invest in affordable inserts with removable covers to test new colors. If your couch is a solid neutral, this is also a fun way to bring in an unexpected and playful pattern without overwhelming the space.

Lamps can also bring color into an otherwise neutral room. Not sure how a specific color will look in your home, but want to give it a shot? Find a lamp at a thrift store (just make sure the wiring is in good condition), and give it a fresh coat of paint! Once you find the ideal base, invest in a shade that looks good with it.

And, of course, you can always paint the space itself. That's right, paint those walls! If you want most of the room to stay neutral, then all you really need is an accent wall. I know it sounds bold, but think of it this way: it's cheaper, easier, and faster to paint over just one wall. If you're nervous about the change (or need to change back before you move out), try a color that complements the neutrals but will be easy to cover up, like a peach or pastel pink.

### GO GEOMETRIC

*Just because you aren't working with bright and saturated color doesn't mean you can't have a bold design. Combining high-contrast neutrals (like, say, black and white) creates a visual pop without any hue whatsoever. This patterned carpet makes a strong statement without clashing with the rest of the room. Balancing it out with bright white walls keeps the look from being overwhelming and allows for little bursts of accent colors to peek through and shine.*

## BOUNCE OFF BASIC WALLS

*Whether an intentional choice or just the result of a landlord who won't let you repaint, neutral walls can provide an excellent backdrop to colorful accessories and even allow you to broaden your scheme to the entire rainbow if you want. Show off brightly hued supplies (or other full-spectrum collections of accessories) against a tame wall color.*

## BE BRIGHT WITH WHITE

*Whites, off-whites, and eggshells do not have to be blah! Against clean bright walls and carpet, a bold, saturated piece, like this royal-blue couch, demands attention and contrasts nicely. The vibrant accent yellow shines even brighter thanks to the reflected light of the white.*

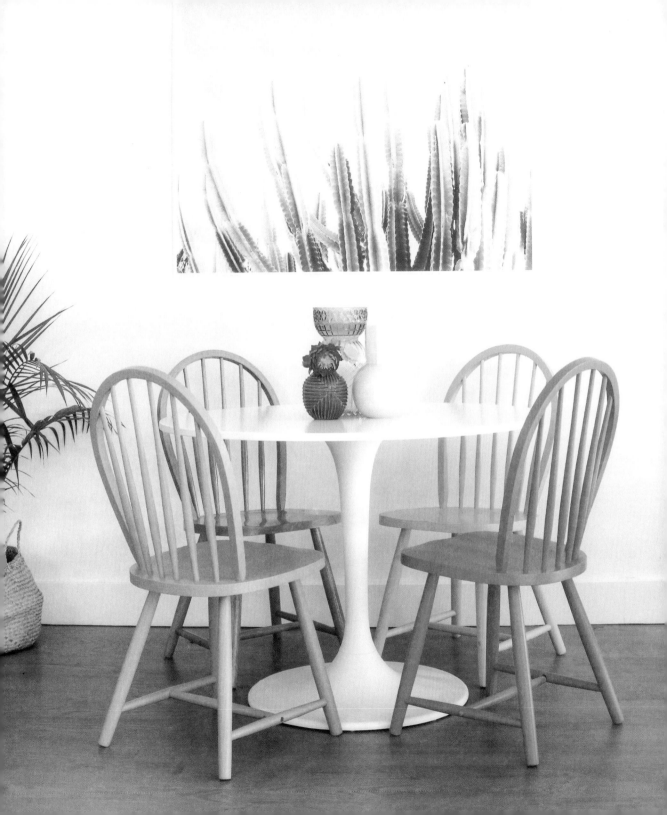

# Chapter Two

# THE DINING ROOM

This is the place where friends gather, food is eaten, and drinks start flowing. Aside from the delicious dishes, one thing guests will be talking about after a meal is the attention to detail you lavish on your table. These projects will make your dining room feel unique and oh so Instagram worthy.

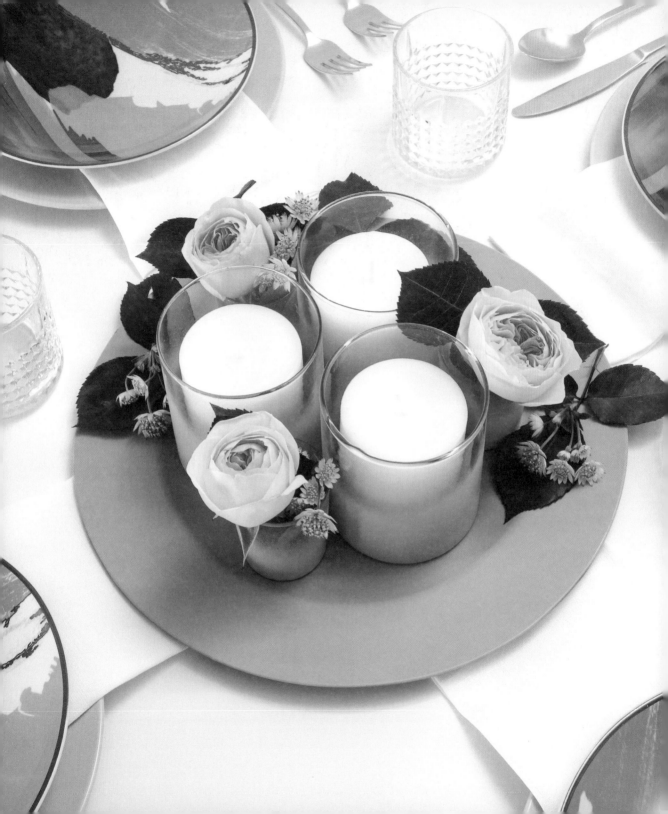

# TWO QUICK
# CENTERPIECES

When having guests for dinner, the last thing you want to do after spending so much time and energy cooking is worry about making a tablescape. But I promise—you don't have to be Martha Stewart to have both great food and a cute table! In fact, you can create gorgeous, colorful accessories in under fifteen minutes with items you already have on hand. Not sure you can pull it all together? Here are two projects that will convince you otherwise.

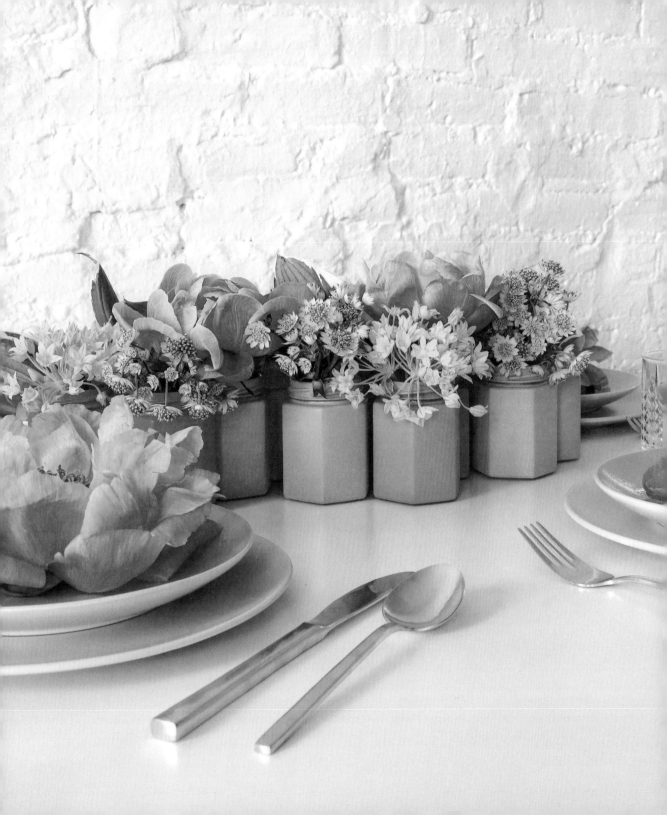

# OMBRÉ VASES

1. Clean the jars completely. You can buy new jars that are all the same size and shape, or opt for old jars you've saved in anticipation of your dinner party. Soak them in warm, soapy water and scrub with a sponge to remove labels. For tough label residue, Goo Gone or nail polish remover should do the trick. Line up the clean and dry jars on cardboard or a drop cloth in an outdoor location (or your garage).

2. Spray-paint the outside of each jar completely. To create an ombré rainbow, choose 3 or 4 colors that are next to one another on the color wheel, paint each jar one color, and then arrange them in color order when ready to display; this is a great way to create a warm or cool tablescape that matches the rest of your decor. If you want more of a gradual, gradient effect across all the vases, place the jars close together as you paint so that some of the colors speckle on to the others.

3. Let the paint dry completely outdoors. When ready to display, fill with flowers or foraged greens, and arrange in a row in the center of the table. Spot clean and wash by hand as needed.

Glass jars

Dish soap and sponge

Goo Gone or nail polish remover (to remove labels)

Cardboard or drop cloth

Spray paint in at least 3 colors

Flowers or greens

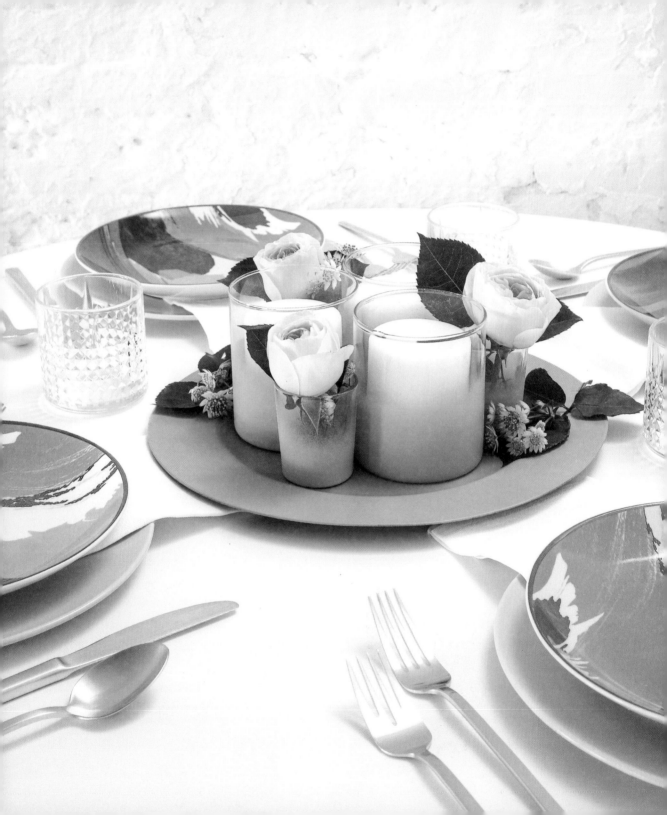

# CANDLE CENTERPIECE

1. Lay the clean and dry tray or plate on cardboard or a drop cloth in an outdoor location (or your garage). Spray-paint the top surface entirely. Let dry, then repeat on the back.

2. If you'd like to bring in additional colors, paint your glass votives in a constrasting hue while the tray is drying. I went for a subtle look and only sprayed the bottom half of each votive. For a similar effect, place the votive on cardboard or a drop cloth and spray-paint around the vase, partly painting the drop cloth so that the paint speckles up the side. Let dry.

3. Once everything is dry, arrange the votives on the tray, fill with candles, and surround with flowers. You can also add loose greenery to fill any open spots. Just keep the candles in mind and avoid placing anything too close to the flames!

4. To preserve color vibrancy, spot-clean by hand.

## MATERIALS

Tray or charger plate that fits your table

Cardboard or drop cloth

Spray paint in 2 or 3 colors

Glass votives in varying sizes, enough to fill your tray or plate

Candles, flowers, and loose greenery

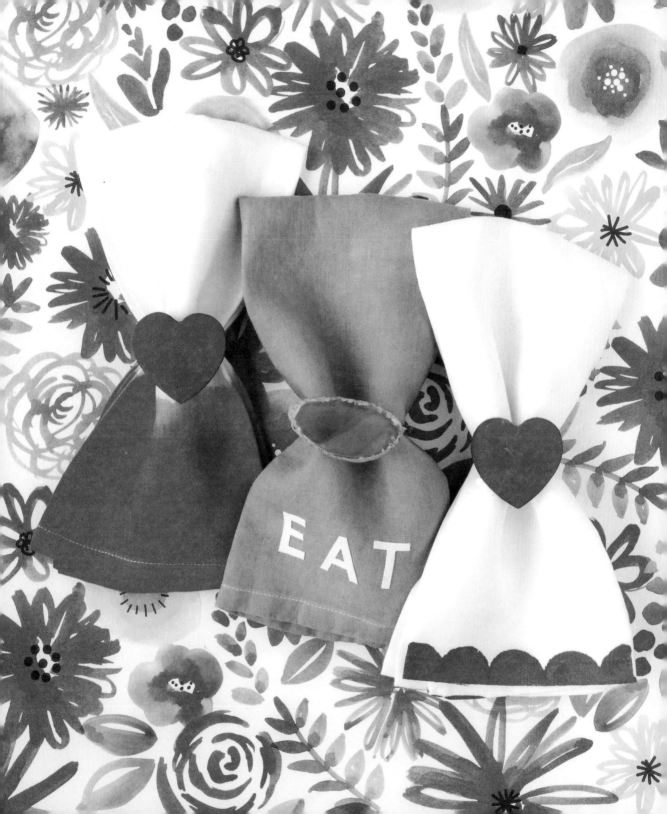

# THREE PRETTY NAPKINS

There are many ways to customize your table with crafts, but the one that allows the most creative freedom is the DIY decorated napkin. Plain cotton napkins are so affordable that you could create lovely sets for everyday use or go all-out and match them to your dinner-party decor. No matter what's on the menu, napkins are the one thing your guests are guaranteed to use during the meal, so why not make them look nice? (Cloth napkins are also more environmentally friendly than paper—a nice bonus.) The possibilities are endless, but here are a few easy ideas to get you started.

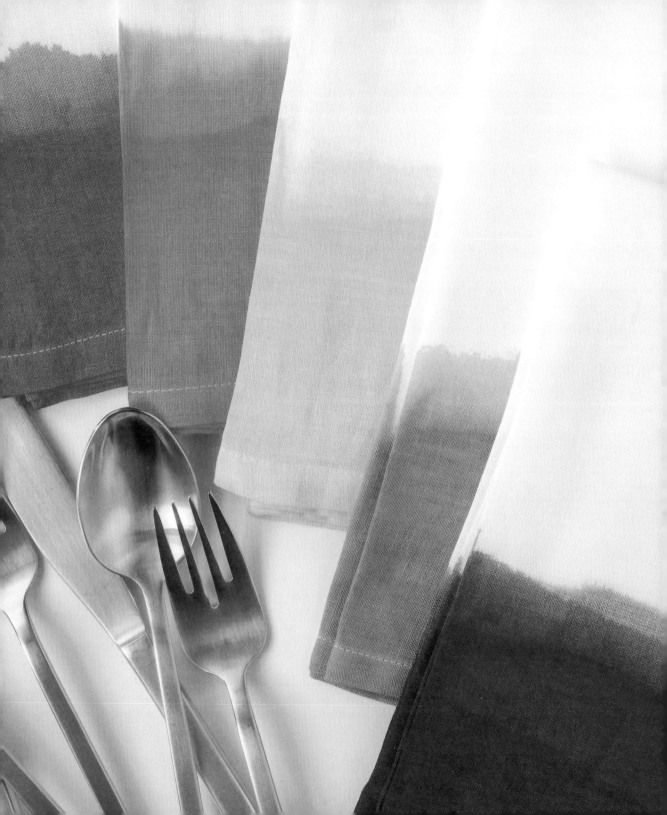

# DIP-DYED NAPKINS

1. Prepare a dye bath: Fill the bowl with hot water, then pour in the dye, following the manufacturer's instructions for proportions, and stir.

2. Fold each napkin the way you plan to display it on the table. Dip the edge of the folded napkin about halfway into the dye bath for a few seconds, then lift it out partially and lay the napkin over the side of the bowl, leaving the ends in to darken.

3. Let the napkin sit in the dye bath for about 10–15 minutes. Personally, I think dyeing is like a good cocktail: the stronger the better. You can check on the color's progress by lifting the napkin out of the dye for a few seconds; just be sure to return it at the same level for even color distribution. (And do keep in mind that the color you see now is darker than it will be when dry.)

4. When the color is to your liking, remove the napkin from the dye and rinse it in cold water until the water runs clear, taking care not to get dye runoff on the white half of the napkin.

5. Repeat with the remaining napkins, creating a new dye bath for each color. Wash the napkins with warm water and detergent (I always do this separately from light-colored clothes, just to be safe) and dry in the dryer. Iron, fold, and store until your next dinner party.

## MATERIALS

Bowl or tub

Liquid fabric dye (such as Rit) in a variety of colors

White cotton napkins

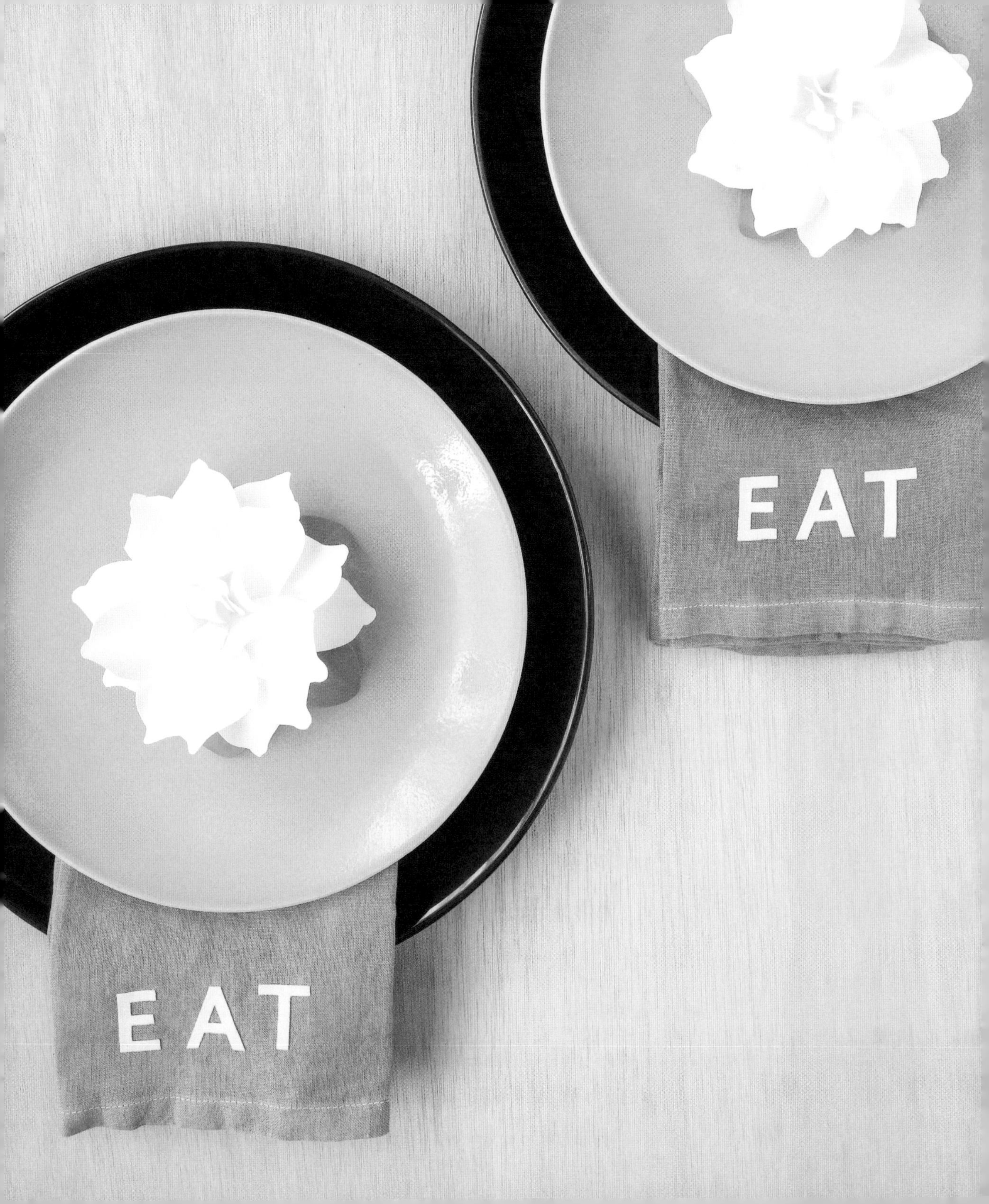
EAT
EAT

# IRON-ON NAPKINS

1. If you want to use dyed napkins for this project, follow the instructions for "Dip-Dyed Napkins" on page 75.

2. Decide where to put the letters: To get the placement just right, iron and fold the napkins the way you plan to display them on the table before affixing the letters to ensure that they will be visible on the finished project. It helps to use a ruler to keep the letters straight, level, and evenly spaced, especially if you're making a matching set of napkins.

3. Preheat your iron according to the iron-on package directions. With the letters arranged on the napkin, place the scrap cloth over the letters, making sure not to move them. Hold the iron in place for about 60 seconds (or as long as recommended by the package directions). Remove cloth, flip the napkin, and iron again. If the letters still aren't sticking, just iron them again until they do (you shouldn't have to do so more than once or twice).

4. Repeat with the remaining napkins. Let cool and you're done! Be sure to wash the napkins according to the package directions (typically in cold water with a gentle detergent) to preserve the iron-on letters.

Cotton napkins or Dip-Dyed Napkins (page 75)

Iron-on letters

Ruler

Scrap piece of cloth

Iron and ironing board

*To make your tablescape more playful, accent your napkins with iron-on letters! Choose a custom phrase if you're hosting a themed dinner party or opt for a short motto, or even your initials, for daily use.*

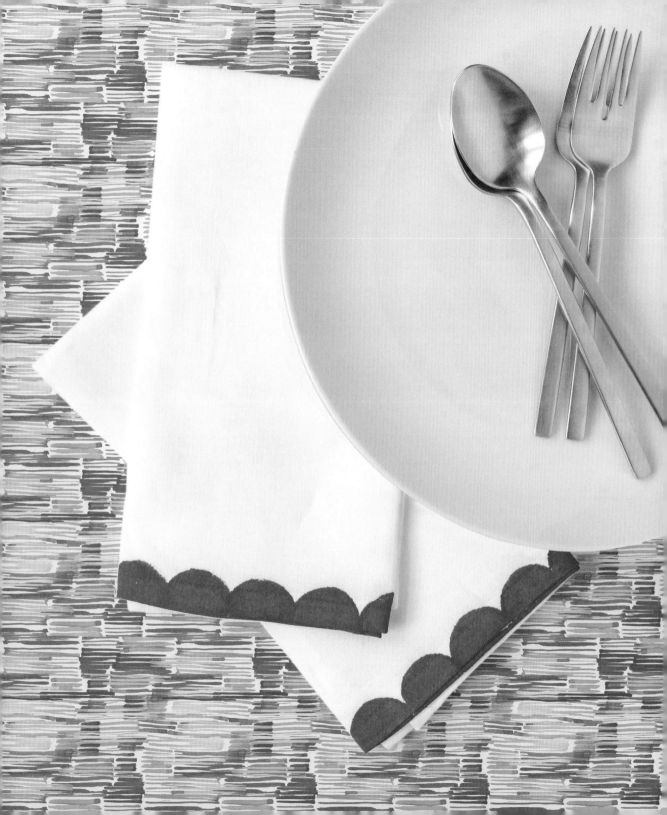

# SCALLOPED NAPKINS

## INSTRUCTIONS

1. If the napkin is creased or wrinkled, iron it to smooth out the fabric. Spread newspaper on your work surface and lay the unfolded copy on top.

2. Pour a small amount of fabric paint onto the paper plate. Dip the pouncer in the paint and make a few practice scallops on scrap paper, by keeping half of the circle on the napkin and half on the newspaper, until you get the hang of it.

3. Napkin time! Apply more paint to the pouncer and dab the scallop pattern along the napkin's top edge like you practiced in step 2.

4. Repeat until you've gone around the top and bottom edges of the napkin, then repeat with the remaining napkins. Once dry, heat-set the paint either in the dryer for 30 minutes or by placing a clean cloth over the painted area and ironing on the cotton setting (usually one of the highest settings). Then just fold and display on your table!

## MATERIALS

Cotton napkins

Iron and ironing board (if needed)

Newspaper

Fabric paint

Paper plate or paint palette

Scrap paper

Foam pouncer (available at craft stores and online)

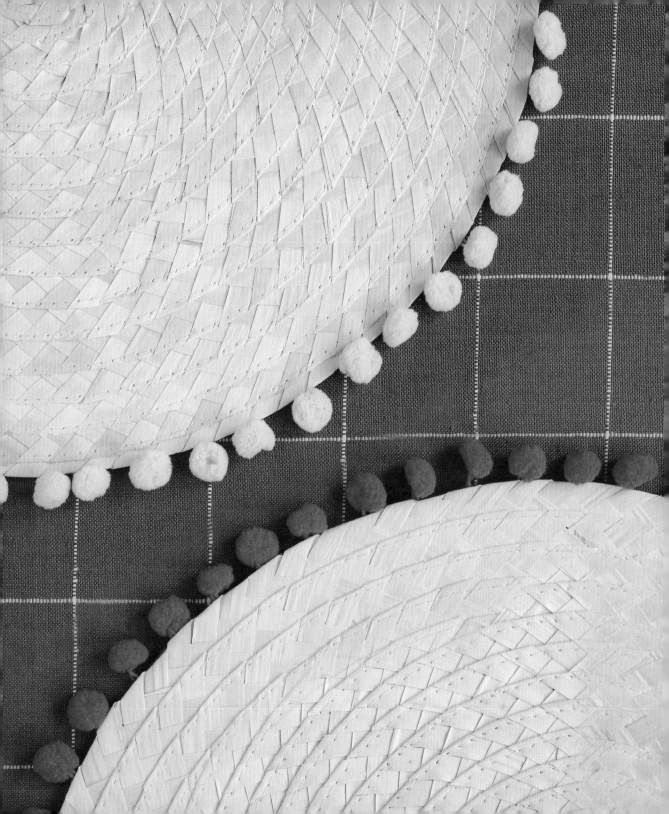

# EMBELLISHED PLACEMATS

The odds of you pulling out placemats on a daily basis are unlikely. You're probably planning on eating and watching Netflix later tonight. (Or maybe that's just me!) But for those times when you feel a little fancy, whether you're on your own or entertaining friends, one-of-a-kind placemats are the perfect way to add a little whimsy to your table. And really, what's cuter than pom-pom fringe?

*You can find simple woven placemats at just about any home-goods store, and pom-pom trim is available at most craft stores and online. (I used 1"—this means my trim measured one inch from the base of the pom to the edge of the trim.) To keep trim in place, spot-clean placemats with a damp towel as needed.*

1 Cut a length of pom-pom trim long enough to go around the edges of your placemat, with a little extra at the end. (If your placements are rectangular, you can cut separate pieces for each side.)

2 With the placemat faceup, position the trim under the edges to ensure that the pom-poms stick out the side.

3 Once you've figured out placement, turn the placemat over (so you're working on the back) and use the hot-glue gun to affix the trim around the edges. Glue all the way around the mat. Snip off excess trim and you're done! It really is as easy as that!

# SALT & PEPPER SHAKER MAKEOVER

Masking tape

Plastic wrap

White ceramic salt
and pepper shakers

"S" and "P" removable
vinyl stickers

Cardboard

Spray paint in varying shades

Clear acrylic sealant

Salt and pepper shakers may be a small detail on your table, but since both you and your dinner guests are almost guaranteed to use them, why not make them a conversation starter? Gradient spray paint is a great way to add a mini burst of color to your tablescape, and the look can be achieved with just a few quick spritzes.

*For this set of shakers, I used pink, orange, and yellow for one, and teal, blue, and green for the other, so that each shaker shows off a subtle hint of color gradient. I recommend testing your palette on paper to make sure you like the look before beginning to paint.*

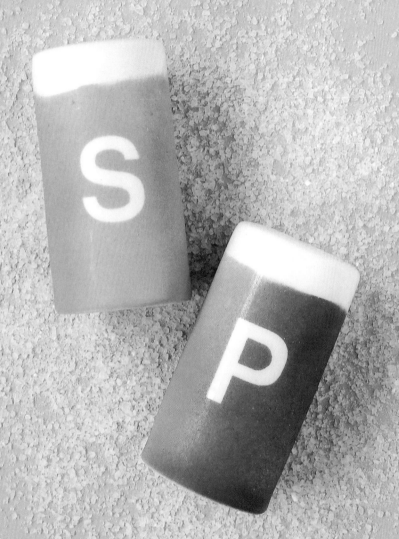

1. Tape over the top half of both shakers—at least half an inch. Because the seasonings are sprinkled on food, you don't want to paint the area where they come out! Same goes for the bottom where you refill; leave that surface free of paint by taping over it before spraying. Depending on the shape and size of your shakers, you may also want to use plastic wrap to mask out space.

2. Place stickers wherever you'd like! After you paint the shakers and peel off the stickers, the space behind them will be white, letting you tell your salt from your pepper. Make sure that both stickers are at the same height so they match when paired on your table.

3. Set one shaker on a piece of cardboard in a well-ventilated area. Start painting with the lightest color first: instead of pointing the spray directly at the shaker, point it more toward the cardboard and make a quick, indirect burst around the base of the shaker. Cover one vertical section with your first color, then repeat with the rest of your colors, going from lightest to dark.

4. Let dry, then peel away the letter (but not the tape or plastic wrap) and apply a quick coat of clear acrylic sealant.

5. Let the shakers dry completely, remove tape and/or plastic wrap, set on your table, and season away!

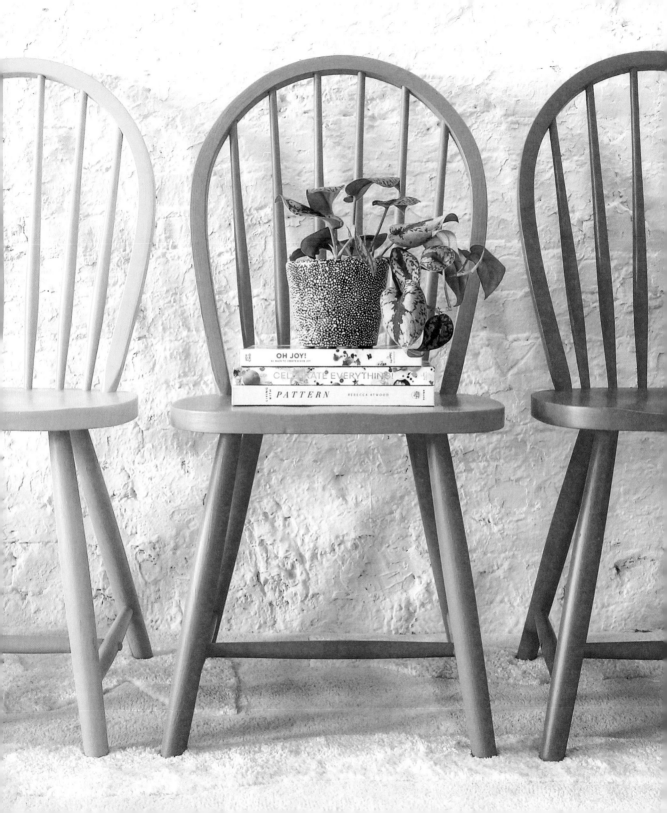

# PAINTED
# CHAIR SET

Wooden chairs

Sandpaper (if needed)

Lint-free cloth

Interior paint (in flat finish)

Paintbrushes (one for each paint color)

Gallon zip-top bag

Furniture wax (such as Annie Sloan brand)

Wax brush

We've all seen those wooden dining chairs clustered at the thrift store. You know the kind I'm talking about: the ones that look like they were in your parents' basement for years. The ones you've probably walked past time and again (don't worry, I'm guilty of this, too). The ones that are functional but just sooo boring. With a dash of color, you can give them new life, and hopefully a new home—with you!

*Not only is this project a one-of-a-kind way to add major color to your dining room, it's also affordable. You don't even have to buy all the same style: with the right color scheme, even mismatched chairs will look like a lovely set. At home improvement stores, you can pick up sample sizes of just about any paint color for under $5, perfect for the multicolor route. If you're opting for all the same color, upgrade to a quart or gallon. The only real trick with this project is patience.*

1. Prep the chairs. If there's a thick glossy finish or layers of paint on the surface, you'll need to sand them until clean and smooth. (If you want to avoid a lot of work, buy unfinished chairs.) Using a damp lint-free cloth, wipe off the chairs so you're not painting over dirt or dust.

2. Brush a coat of paint onto each chair. For a smoother and brighter finish, you'll most likely need two coats. To keep your paintbrush from drying out between coats, place it in the zip-top bag and seal. That should keep the bristles soft and the ends wet with paint. Let the chairs dry completely—this can take as little as one to three hours, but it's best to leave them overnight.

3. Once dry, seal each chair with wax, following the manufacturer's instructions. That will help guard your paint job from any scratches or nicks from daily wear and tear, so it's worth the extra step. After the wax has set, your dining room table will have gotten a colorful facelift, just like that!

# How to Set a Charming Table

For get-togethers and sit-down meals that deserve more than paper plates, wow your guests with a beautiful table! When paired with DIYs from this book, a gorgeous, colorful arrangement will materialize in no time at all. To channel your inner Martha (and keep you from googling "how to set the table" time and again), here are a few tablescaping tricks you'll memorize in a snap!

## STOCKING UP

When you think about a set table, you might envision formal events, fancy restaurants, or stuffy old-fashioned rules. But nowhere is it written that you have to set your grandma's table! With bright colors, fun patterns, interesting glassware, and Instagrammable flatware, you can create a lovely dining experience. (And honestly, your guests will care less about proper fork placement if the setting is beautiful!) Here are basic pieces to consider investing in:

**PLATES:** salad, dinner, bread, and dessert. Chargers are optional and can be swapped out for placemats. If mixing and matching plates, consider how they will look stacked. If shopping at a flea market or antiques store, choose different styles that have a similar color or pattern that match.

**GLASSWARE:** water, red wine, white wine, and champagne. You may also want mugs if serving coffee or tea with dessert.

**SERVING DISHES:** bowls (both small, for individual servings of soup, and large, for salads or bread for the table), platters, and slabs/cutting boards for cheese. Don't forget the corresponding serving utensils!

**FLATWARE:** forks (salad and dinner), knives (butter and steak), and spoons (soup, dessert, and demitasse if you're fancy). Nowadays you can find flatware in more than just silver tones—keep an eye out for rose gold, copper, and gold. Some metallics are hand wash only, so you may want to save those for special occasions.

## LAYING IT ALL OUT

Even though you're not beholden to the past, it's good to know basic table-setting etiquette in order to mix the modern with the traditional. The simplest, most important rule is this: forks go on the left, knives to the immediate right of the plate (blades turned in, please), and spoons to the right of the knives. Although there's a "traditional" spread of silverware for formal dinners, in reality, the meal you're serving can dictate what you do and do not need on the table. (For example, if you're not serving soup or chili, there's no need for soup spoons.)

For meals with multiple courses, an easy way to remember where the silverware goes (because that's really the hardest part) is to put the utensils used first on the outside of the setting, so that your guests work their way in toward the plate for each course. Typically, the soup and salad courses are served first, so the soup spoon (usually with a bigger, rounder bowl) and salad fork (like a dinner fork, but with shorter tines) will be on the outside of the place setting, with the dinner fork and knife closer to center. Again, if you aren't serving soup or salad, those utensils don't have to be on the table; but providing an extra fork and spoon means that you and your guests don't have to use the same utensil for multiple dishes and risk clashing flavors. If you're serving coffee or a spoonable dessert, you'll also want an additional non-soup spoon. And if you're serving steak, chops, or anything that needs serious cutting, provide sharp serrated knives.

The same goes for plates: set out whatever corresponds to your meal. The traditional order is a dinner plate (larger) on the bottom, and a salad

on fun and unique place settings. (That's honestly the real reason I like to host, because in no way is it about the food I'm capable of making!) Creating an inviting display is all about accessories. You can use a napkin to dress up your plates if you feel like folding it fancy, or you can layer it between the salad and dinner plate. (To stick with tradition, place the napkin on the left of the plates, under the forks.) Add place-card holders or special favors and your table will instantly look straight out of a magazine.

That's all there is to it! After a few parties, you'll nail the basics and can play around with crafting your perfect table. Bring in more pops of color with decorative items like tapered candles, table runners/cloths, and centerpieces. You can even customize each setting by decorating chairs with ribbons, greenery, or a small floral bouquet (that guests can take with them). Making the delicious food is all on you, though!

plate (smaller) on the top, so that the main course doesn't get dressing all over it. Soup bowls, if needed, can go on top of the salad plate. Bread plates (if you have them) should be placed above and to left of the dinner plate.

As for glasses, think of this: When you eat at a restaurant with four people at your table, which hand do you typically grab your glass with? The right, of course! (Sorry, lefties.) And that's exactly where it should go on your table at home, in the right corner of the setting. Water glasses are a must for any meal, and you can set out wineglasses if serving that beverage. If coffee or tea will be served with dessert, wait until the main course has been cleared before setting out mugs to avoid overcrowding the table.

Silverware and plating are just the beginning. One of my favorite things to do for guests is to work

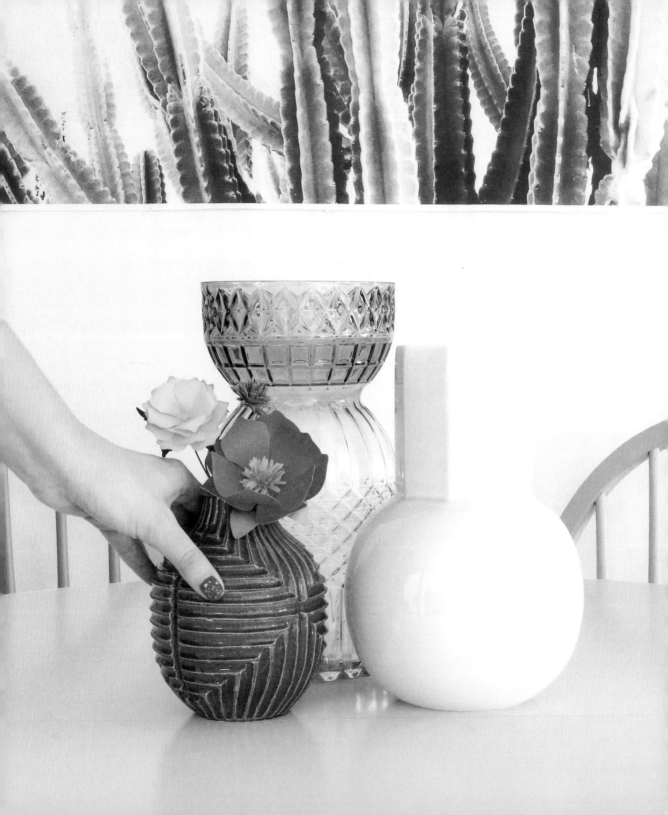

# Warm & Cool Colors

Whether or not we sense it, colors affect the way we feel. Warm colors—the hues within the red to yellow range—pick you up and stimulate you, whereas cool colors—blue through violet—make you feel calm and refreshed. Think of their roles in the natural world: warm colors are linked to sunlight, heat, and fire; cool colors are connected to the sea and sky. However, warm colors aren't restricted to reds, yellows, and oranges; a brown, yellow-green, or tan can have distinctly warm undertones. Similarly, reds with purple undertones, a blue-toned cadmium yellow, and many grays read "cool."

It's always worth considering how you want to feel when you're in the room you're decorating. Paying attention to warm and cool colors and their associated emotions will help you find a balanced, harmonious palette and create a home that makes you happy. Here are a few options to start with:

## WARM COLORS

**YELLOW:** An all-around joyful color. For a bold look, pair a mustard/school-bus hue with pink and mint.

**PINK:** Clearly a personal favorite of mine—it makes a great hair color! Pairs well with brown and olive.

**CORAL:** A softer version of orange that can still be bold. Looks great with white, teal, and yellow.

## COOL COLORS

**COBALT BLUE:** Clashes with very few colors. You can pair with warms like pink and yellow or cools like mint and turquoise.

**FOREST GREEN:** A great rich alternative to black. Pairs well with grays and gold.

**TURQUOISE:** For a softer look, mix with other cools like navy. You can also go bold and tropical with a dash of canary yellow or bright pink.

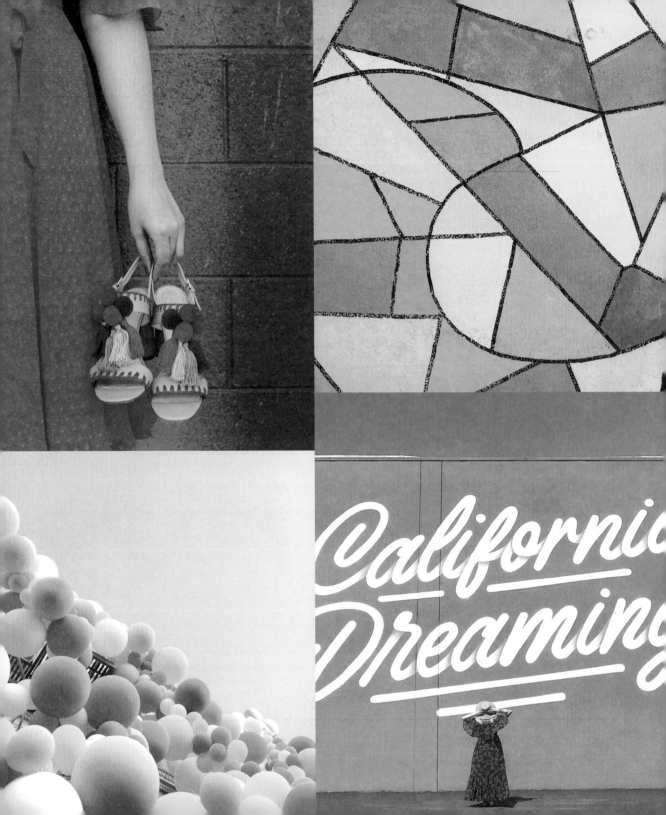

## HOW TO APPLY

Not only can warm and cool colors change how you feel, but they also affect how you perceive space. While it's true that cool colors may help you unwind, they also recede in space, which is great for making a smaller room, like a bathroom, feel larger. By contrast, warm colors tend to jump out of the frame, so they can make a large space feel cozy. Warm colors are also great for rooms that see a lot of social interaction, like the dining room, living room, and kitchen.

For the bedroom, I believe the choice is up to you. You could go with either end of the color spectrum, depending on what you need from this space. If all you want to do when you get home is sleep and de-stress, consider a cool theme. But if a yellow bedroom makes you feel happy when you wake up, then by all means paint yourself a yellow bedroom.

Even if you opt for white walls and a white rug, you can bring in warms and cools with furniture, wall art, and accessories. And if you're picking a palette to help show off your space, remember that lighter hues on walls and floors make any room feel larger. (Sometimes it helps to paint the ceiling to draw the eye upward.)

Experiment with variety and spend some time with each color to determine not only how it makes you feel, but also how it looks in the space throughout the day (and year). If you're considering painting a wall an intense red, pick up a sample and test it. Live with the color for a while to see how it looks and changes in different light: golden evening light will warm up everything it hits; bluer morning light (or light from lamps) can cool things off. You may love that red in the evening but dislike how the sun reflects off it during the day, so it may be better suited to your bedroom than your kitchen or office.

### TAKE IT OUTSIDE

*Warm palettes work wonderfully outside and can lend an energizing, vacation-y feel to your space. Peachy pinks, corals, and sunset oranges evoke a tropical getaway or a gorgeous Spanish villa and look great in an ombré to boot. Try this on the Painted Chair Set (page 87) using outdoor furniture and a weatherproof sealant for an instant escape.*

## LET THE SUNSHINE IN

*Most people stick with tame browns, blacks, or dark blues for their exterior paint—but why not be literally warm and inviting? An energizing lemony yellow brightens walls and gives the entire house a must-see curb appeal. Keeping it simple with just one look-at-me warm color avoids a too-wacky, overwhelming palette—you don't want to be that house. (Some communities may have restrictions on what colors are permitted on exteriors, so check first!)*

## LIGHT IT ALL UP

*Purchasing special colored bulbs is always fun for a party, but even in your everyday use, it's important to consider lighting. Standard incandescent bulbs release a warmer light, while energy-efficient compact fluorescents and LEDs typically release a cooler, bluer light (as do "daylight" or "natural light" incandescents). Neither one is inherently better, but consider your decor: brighter, bluer light might work well to energize the kitchen but could be too stimulating in the bedroom (light near to the spectrum of daylight sends "wake up!" signals to your brain).*

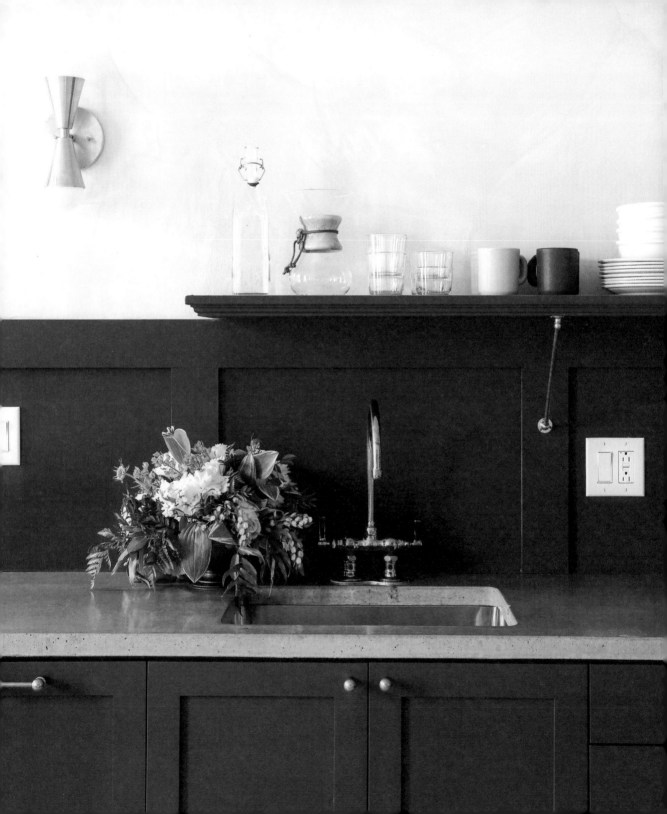

# Chapter Three

# THE KITCHEN

The kitchen is the perfect place to channel your inner Martha Stewart. It's an essential part of your home, whether you love to cook or not. And even if the latest recipe you're testing is a flop, at least you'll be surrounded by successful craft projects when you call to order a pizza!

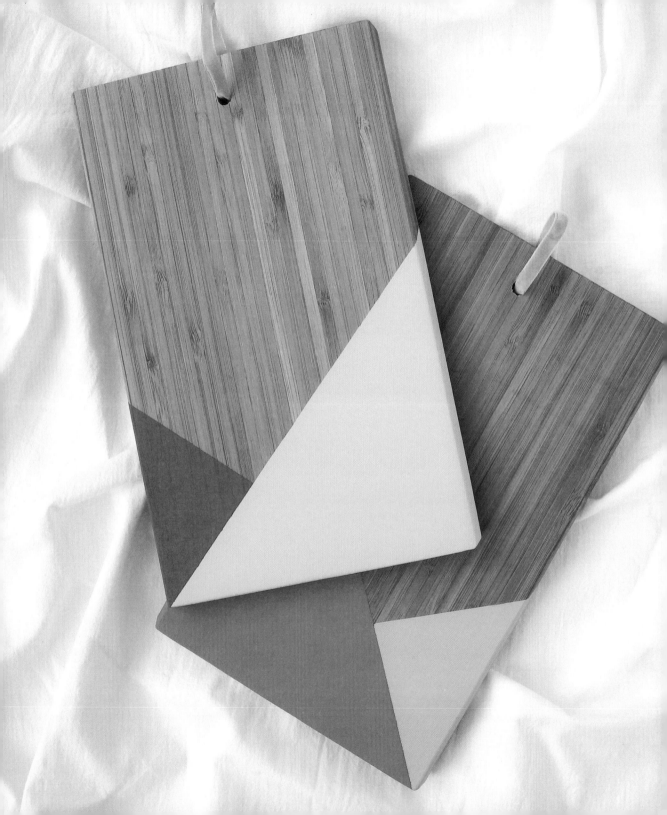

# COLOR-BLOCKED TRIVETS

MATERIALS

Small wood slab or cutting board

Measuring tape

Pencil

Scrap wood

Power drill and safety goggles

Painter's tape

Acrylic paint

Paintbrush

Paper plate or paint palette

Clear acrylic sealant

Cording or ribbon

Let's be honest: when it comes to cooking, things in the kitchen can get hectic. More often than not, I find myself taking something out of the oven right before it burns and grabbing the nearest towel or pot holder to protect my counters. The good news is that I found a fun and easy DIY solution (and no, it's not just ordering takeout instead).

These color-block trivets are cute enough to hang on the wall or set directly on the countertop so you don't have to fumble with hot pots and pans. Plus, if you're cooking for guests, they can also double as table decor. It's a win-win, my friends, and takes only a few simple steps to complete!

*You can buy a piece of wood, cut it to size (or have it cut), and sand it, but if you're looking to save time, use a cutting board instead. As far as drilling, this is as easy as it gets! If you're inexperienced with power tools, buy scrap wood to practice on. Be sure to wear safety glasses and take your time—there's no rush!*

1   Measure and mark with a pencil a place in the center of the wood, near the top, about an inch from the edge. This is where you'll drill a hole for your cord loop.

2   Select a drill bit that will create a hole large enough to thread your cord through (I used a ¼-inch bit). Place a thick piece of scrap wood underneath the board to avoid puncturing your work surface. Drill a hole all the way through your board where you marked it, stopping when you hit the scrap wood. (Remember to wear safety goggles when drilling.)

3   Starting in one corner, tape off an angle. Don't forget to wrap around the sides! (For an extra-crisp paint line, run your fingernail over the tape after it's in place.) Paint the taped-off section, starting at the tape and brushing away from it. Let dry for a few minutes, then remove the tape.

4   Repeat step 3, taping off a second area and painting with another color to create a blocked look.

5   Once all the painted areas are dry, spray the board (front and sides) with a coat of clear acrylic sealant and set aside until dry.

6   Tie a length of cord or ribbon through the hole, knot it to form a loop, and you're done!

# RAINBOW-SCALLOPED SUGAR AND FLOUR CANISTERS

## MATERIALS

Containers for storing sugar and flour (ceramic or plastic work great)

Permanent adhesive-backed vinyl

Large circle hole punch

Scissors

When sweets are waiting to be baked (and, more important, eaten), who has time to spend on a project? Nobody, that's who. That's why this quick craft is perfect! You can update your sugar and flour containers in minutes with no paint and no mess. In just a few simple steps, your kitchen will be a little more colorful and you'll be on your way to dunking a warm chocolate chip cookie into milk, as you should be.

*Instead of writing* sugar *and* flour *on your containers, try using different color palettes for each one to distinguish which is which. To create the colorful shapes that make up the scalloped pattern, you'll want a hole punch that's nice and sharp to pierce through the vinyl.*

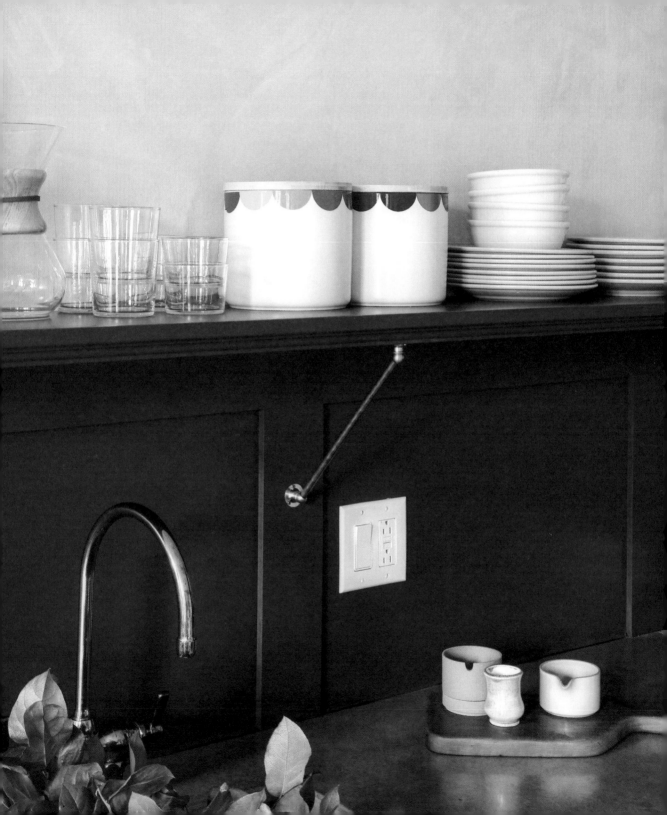

1   Using the hole punch, punch circles out of your vinyl. Cut each circle in half using the scissors to create a scallop.

2   Peel the backing off the vinyl and affix a half circle to your container, keeping the flat edge of the vinyl against the rim and smoothing with your finger to remove air bubbles.

3   Continue applying half circles until you've gone all the way around the container—and that's it! Although the vinyl is permanent, I suggest hand-washing your containers to preserve the design.

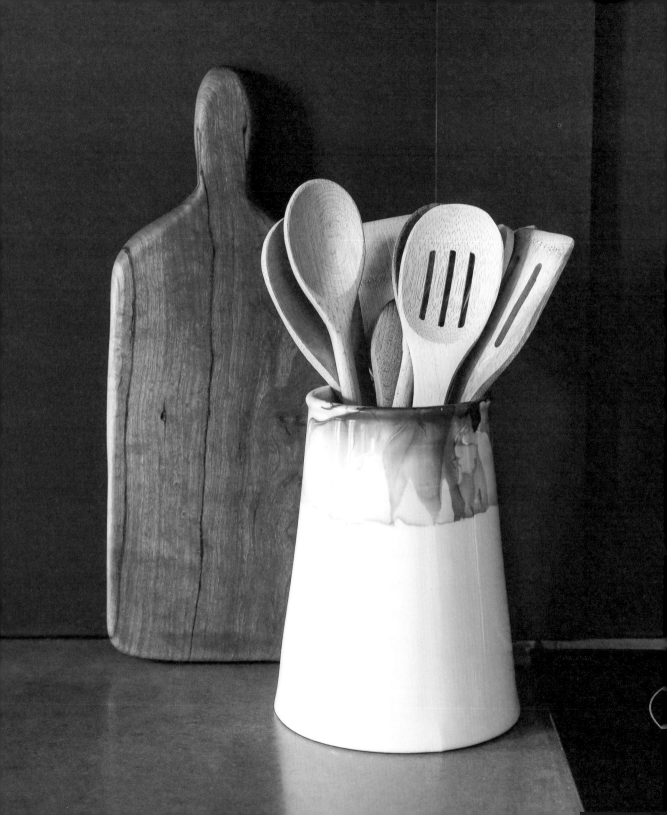

# MARBLE-DIPPED UTENSIL HOLDER

Deep tub, bowl, or bucket

Ceramic utensil holder

Nail polish in various colors (not quick-dry)

Craft stick

Everyone has a utensil holder on the kitchen counter, and for the most part we think nothing of them. But just because they serve a purpose doesn't mean you have to settle for a plain, colorless container! If you want to add some unexpected color to your counter-tops, then this project is the way go. Plus, once you learn to marble, it'll be really hard to stop!

*The trick to successful marbling is working fast. I've found that it helps to take the cap off all the nail polishes, then pour them into the hot water at the same time with one hand as you swirl a pattern with the other. I suggest doing a couple test runs before marbling your utensil holder. Finally, be sure to work in a well-ventilated area because there will be fumes!*

1   Fill the tub, bowl, or bucket with hot water. Whichever vessel you use, make sure it's deep enough to cover as much of the utensil holder as you want to marble. (If you're marbling flatter objects, you'll need something that's only a few inches deep. Keep in mind for future projects!) Note that in the future you can use this container *only* for marbling/painting since the nail polish will drop to the bottom and stick there—so don't use your nice baking bowls!

2   Pour the polish in the water and use your craft stick to gently stir and mix the colors to create a marbled effect. Immediately dip in your utensil holder. I suggest going straight down from the center of the polish bath to evenly coat all the way around.

3   Pull the utensil holder out of the water and let dry. You can dab off excess water, just be careful not to smudge the design.

4   Let the container dry completely, then fill with utensils.

# BRIGHT HANGING PLANTER

MATERIALS

Plastic container

Goo Gone (if needed)

Scissors

Spray paint

Cardboard or newspaper

Knife

Cutting board

String/cord for hanging

Plant and potting soil

Aside from a few food splatters on the wall, my guess is that your kitchen doesn't have a ton of color. And though you probably want plants in there (because where doesn't a plant look great?), countertops are usually dedicated to appliances and food prep. That's where this hanging planter comes in to save the day! It can decorate your space without giving pets tasty foliage and flowers to chew up. Make one for your favorite plant, or whip up an entire set for an indoor vertical herb garden. The materials are everyday items you likely already have on hand.

*You can use just about any plastic container for this project—just make sure the plastic is thin enough to cut and punch holes in. (I used an old dish soap container.) And whenever you're using sharp tools, please use caution and protect your hands!*

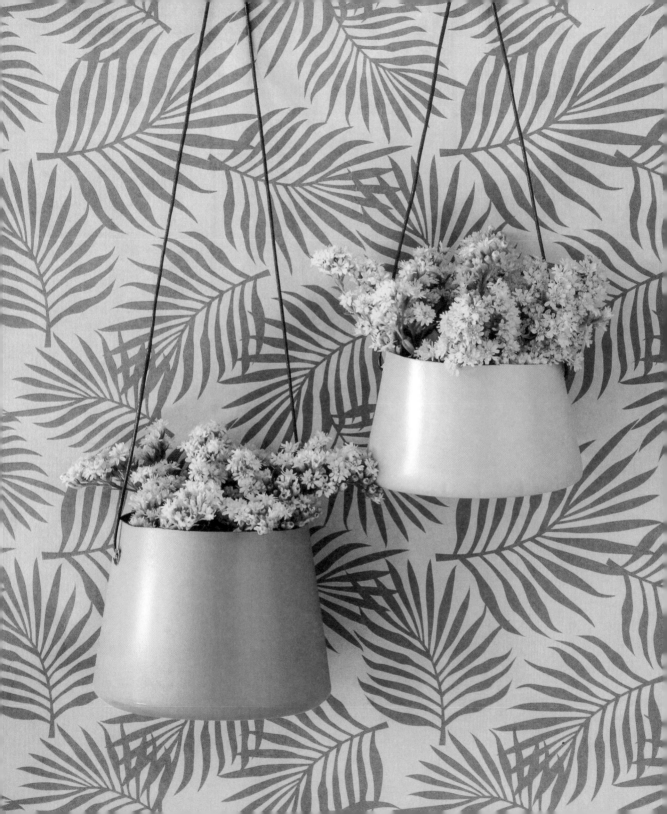

1  Wash and dry your container, then peel off any labels. If necessary, remove sticky residue with Goo Gone so that it doesn't show under the paint.

2  Using sharp scissors or a knife, cut the top off the container so that you're left with an open base.

3  Puncture two holes in the container near the top, one opposite the other: use the tip of a knife to pierce the plastic on a cutting board, expanding the holes as necessary so the cord will pass through.

4  In a well-ventilated area, lay down cardboard or newspaper. Place container on the covered work surface and spray-paint it inside and out. Let dry.

5  Thread the cording through the holes and knot on the inside of the container. Trim excess cord, fill the container with your plant and soil, and enjoy!

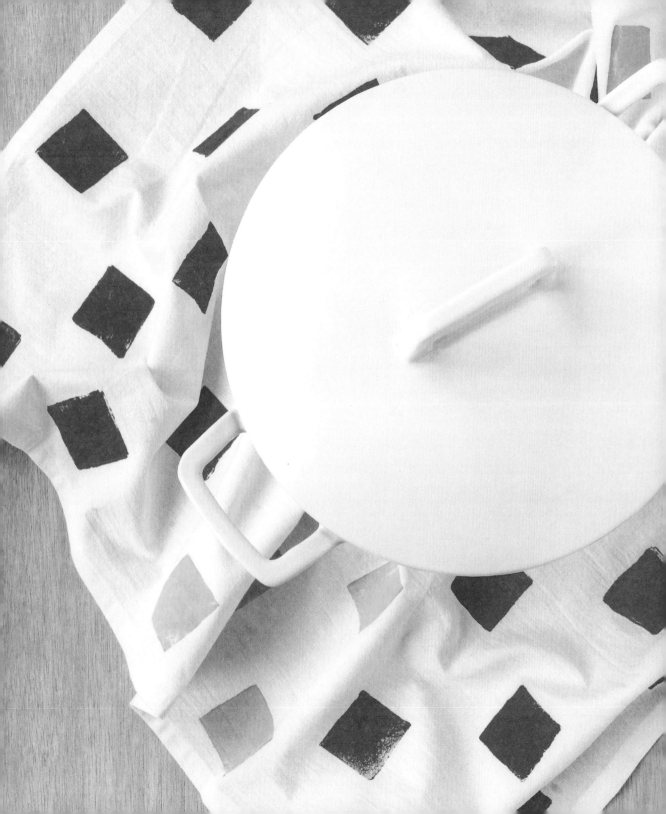

# RAINBOW-STAMPED DISH TOWELS

Flour sack (cotton) dish towels

Craft foam

Hot-glue gun

Wood block

Scissors

Cardboard or newspaper

Fabric paint or multi-surface paint

Paper plate or paint container

Paintbrush

Homemade stamps open up a world of creative possibilities. They're perfect for designing custom patterns and are much more affordable than store-bought options. If you have wooden blocks left over from the Mini Photo Blocks project (page 135), then you're already halfway to making your stamp for this one!

*You can of course buy premade stamps in almost any design you can think of, but I like crafting my own simple squares. Make double-sided stamps to save on blocks!*

1  Make your stamp: Use hot glue to affix a piece of craft foam to the wooden block; let dry and then trim foam to the size and shape you want the stamp to be. Remember that the smaller your design, the longer it will take to cover the dish towel.

2  Cover your work surface with cardboard or newspaper in case paint bleeds through. Spread the towel on the covered surface.

3  Pour paint into the paper plate and dip your foam stamp into it. Using the paintbrush, dab on additional paint so that every part of the stamp surface is covered. If you apply too much, the paint may seep out the sides and your design will not be as crisp as it could be. That's where using the brush helps.

4  Stamp your design onto the towel. Leave stamped shapes as is (for a textured look), or fill in white patches with the paintbrush for a solid design. When stamping with multiple colors, instead of stamping the entire towel with each color one at a time, I alternated colors as I worked to make sure stamps of the same color didn't end up side by side. Continue stamping until the towel is covered with your pattern. Repeat on as many towels as you'd like, then let dry overnight.

5  After drying overnight, heat-set the paint. You can either toss the towels in the dryer for 30 minutes, or, with a pressing cloth on top, press a dry iron (no steam) on each towel for 30 seconds at a time, moving from one section to another, until you've set the entire surface.

6  Hang towels on the oven door handle, or tuck them in a drawer and pull out for a little burst of color when needed.

# PHOTO MAGNETS

## MATERIALS

Computer and printer
(for photos)

Photo paper

Craft knife

Small wooden frames, available
at any large craft store

Painter's tape

Paint

Paintbrush

Paper plate or paint palette

Thin-point permanent marker
(optional)

Clear acrylic sealant

Tacky glue

Magnets

E-6000 glue

You did it—you finally took a vacation! Instead of picking up a tacky and overpriced souvenir to remember those days of bliss (I'm talking about you, faux-bikini shirt), try making these travel keepsake magnets from photos of your trip. Not only will they add color to your fridge, but they'll also be a daily reminder of all the fun you had, hopefully motivating you to plan your next getaway. And if you absolutely had to grab a souvenir, you can totally make this project while wearing that tacky faux-bikini shirt and sipping a margarita. I won't judge.

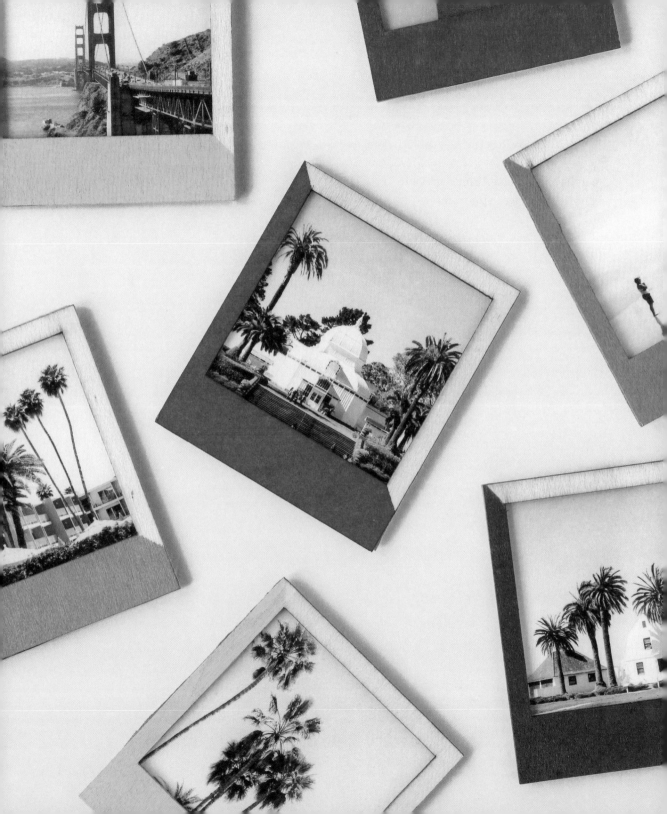

1. Prepare your photos: I printed mine as 4-inch squares and moved the frame until I found the section I liked best; then I cut the photo to size. Print your photos smaller if you want more of the image in the frame.

2. Affix painter's tape to the frame at an angle and paint one section of the frame (as shown). Peel off the tape and let paint dry. If you want to remember where the photo was taken, use the marker to write the date and location on the front before sealing the frame.

3. Coat frame with a layer of clear acrylic sealant and let dry.

4. Flip the frame facedown. Apply a thin layer of tacky glue all around the back of the frame, then position your photo and affix it. Let the glue dry completely—if you rush the drying, you'll have a harder time trimming the edges of your photos!

5. With the craft knife, cut away any part of the photo that's peeking out from behind the frame.

6. Use the E-6000 glue to attach your magnet to the back of the photo and enjoy!

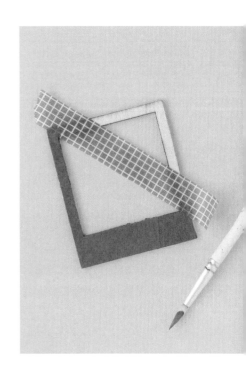

# Creative Ways to Organize Supplies

Nothing slows down a project like a messy craft room. You can't find the supplies you need or even see what you have. Even worse, disorder can limit creativity. When you're too focused on the mess, there's less time to daydream about what you're capable of making—and that's no good.

In an ideal world, we would put away all our tools and tidy up as we work, but that's just not how it happens. Sometimes you have to get a little messy! Instead of forcing yourself to be perfect and neat, try devising a craft storage system that works with you and the way you work.

Here are some tried and true tips that will help you *want* to clean up after a project, allowing you to spend less time tidying and more time doing the important things, like shopping for shoes online.

### 1. FIRST AND FOREMOST, DITCH THE CLUTTER!
I know that as crafters we want to save everything from yogurt lids to old candy tins in the hopes of using them someday. But if you don't have an immediate plan for an item, or if it's not a material you use frequently, don't let it collect dust in your space. Trust me, I know that ribbon scrap is pretty, but the odds of ever using it are low. Once your space is full of tools and materials you turn to regularly, it will be easier to organize.

### 2. SEPARATE YOUR SUPPLIES.
Grouping things by type or function will help you find what you're looking for faster: all the tape in one drawer, all the glues in another, all the brushes in a bin, and so on. This also makes putting materials away easier because you immediately know what goes where without having to find a new place to put it. For miscellaneous items, try grouping them into categories by type of craft if you don't have enough to warrant individual containers.

### 3. WHEN IT COMES TO STORAGE, THINK OUTSIDE THE BOX.
I love open containers for organization. They help me access and put away items quickly while allowing me to display some of

my prettier supplies. For example, mason jars are perfect for corralling paintbrushes and scissors, and wire baskets are great for showing off a washi tape collection. If you've got a small space, consider an over-the-door shoe organizer—you stash supplies in all the compartments.

### 4. NOT SO INTO OPEN STORAGE? TRY LABELING AND DECORATING BOXES INSTEAD. You can paint plain boxes from craft stores, or give an old shoebox a DIY makeover with pretty paper and decoupage.

### 5. MAKE SPACE. You can put your supplies into boxes all you want, but if you don't have a set place to put everything, it will just end up getting disorganized again. Clear a small section of your home, whether a corner or a closet or a shelf on a bookcase, and dedicate it expressly to your supplies. Not only will things be easier to locate when you need them, you're also less likely to mix up non-craft-related items with your supplies. Wall shelves and pegboards are a great solution if you're tight on floor space.

### 6. FIND A WAY TO DISPLAY YOUR SUPPLIES THAT'S AS DECORATIVE AS IT IS FUNCTIONAL. For example, if you're storing paints in a basket instead of loose on a shelf, make sure the tubes are tightly closed and stored upside down. You'll be able to see and grab colors faster, and putting them in rainbow order is always fun to do! Any type of material with a pretty label also looks good grouped together on open shelving.

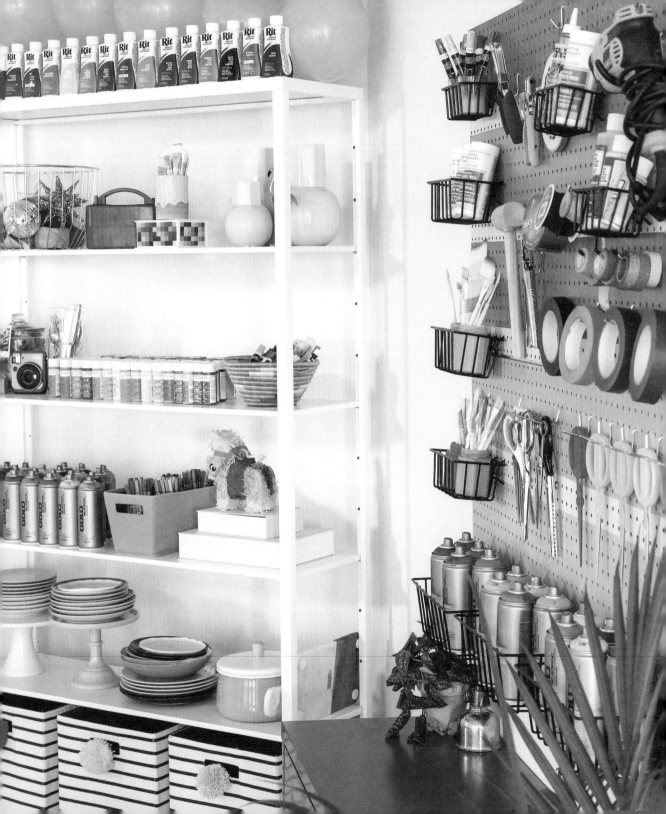

# Bolds & Brights

By now you're familiar with basic color theory, warm and cool colors, neutrals, the works—you're pretty much a color theorist! (Please don't take my job.) But if you're ready to go one step further and dive head-first into full-on color, I am here to support and help you with your decision.

I'm talking bold on bold, color on color. Those deep, vibrant, eye-popping palettes that pack a real punch.

Bold colors are very saturated and have a lot of pigment. Bright colors also have a high saturation but retain enough white to keep them from being too strong to look at for long. Bright colors are usually bold, but bold colors aren't necessarily bright (think of deep blue or green). Regardless, both are colors that grab your attention, perk you up, and make you happy. You can pair them in small doses, maybe as the paint colors for a simple DIY project, or go big and apply them full-scale to an entire room or area of your home (hello, pink couch!). Either way, these pairings are sure to look wonderful, no matter where in your life you decide to let them live.

**PINK + ORANGE + YELLOW:** Bright and warming like a sunset. When paired, these warm colors may also remind you of tropical fruit or a beach vacation, and who doesn't love that?

**TEAL + YELLOW:** The perfect warm and cool color pairing. When side by side, these two colors pull out different values from each other and truly stand out.

**PINK ON PINK:** Because really, you can never have too much pink. Pair different shades, tints, and saturations of pink to create a modern Barbie dreamland.

**NAVY + ORANGE + PINK:** Rich and bold without being over the top. When paired, these colors help each other pop by comparison.

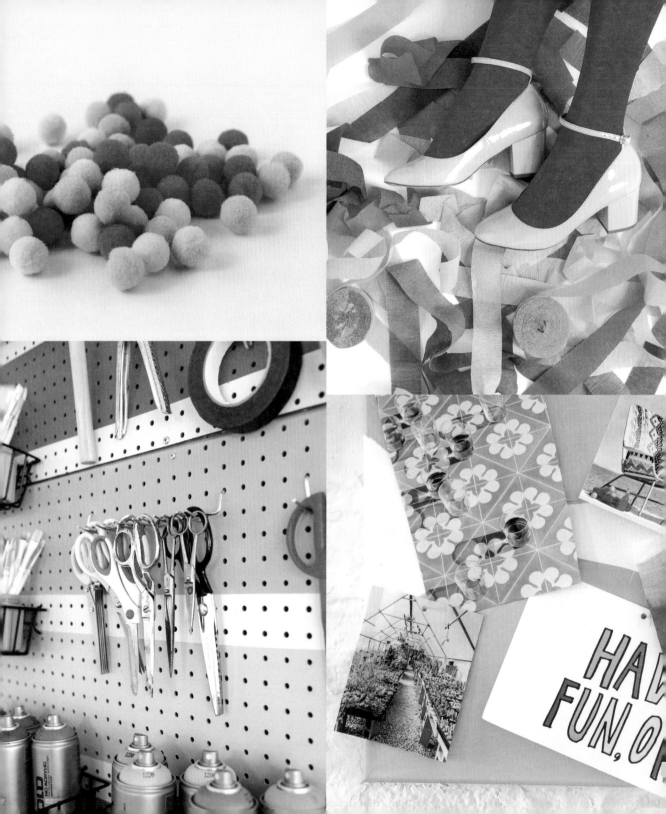

## HOW TO APPLY

Always opt for the most vibrant hue of every color, and match values as best you can. If one color is slightly duller than the other, the brighter one will dominate and you'll end up with a main color and an accent instead of a matched pair. To avoid one color overpowering the other, pick colors with similar richness (intensity) to balance each other out.

One of the main reasons to go bold is to make a statement and attract attention to a room; there's no ignoring these colors, and this certainly isn't a subtle approach to decorating. But by the same token, an all-out palette can easily look super dated (1970s pool party, anyone?). To keep the palette feeling chic and fresh (instead of cheesy or retro), opt for clean lines and modern design. It also helps to bring in metallics like gold for a polished look.

Go bold, have fun!

### MAKE A SOPHISTICATED SPECTRUM

*You* can *use every bold color in the rainbow, and it doesn't have to look totally Lisa Frank. (Although if that's your look, then go for it!) Mixing a little of a brown, gray, white, or black into your paints will push all your colors into the same family even if they are across the color wheel from each other.*

### KEEP IT IN THE FAMILY

*A deep, bold color will naturally play nicely with a tint of the same color. (Plus, you'll only need to pick up two paint colors: your base shade and white!) Adding splotches of the opposite color on top of each color block gives flat colors complimentary texture. Matching footwear is optional!*

## SPRUCE UP WOODEN OBJECTS

*Bold hues go nicely with natural materials like wood, keeping them from feeling dainty or beach-house-y. With these colorful utensils, you can even line them all up to create a fun "box of crayons" vibe, too!*

## GET IT ALL OUTSIDE

*If you're still nervous about bringing such a dramatic look into your home, try it outside for a summer on a balcony or patio. With the carefree nature of the outdoors, and the bright light from the sun, bold color pairings feel totally, well, natural in this setting.*

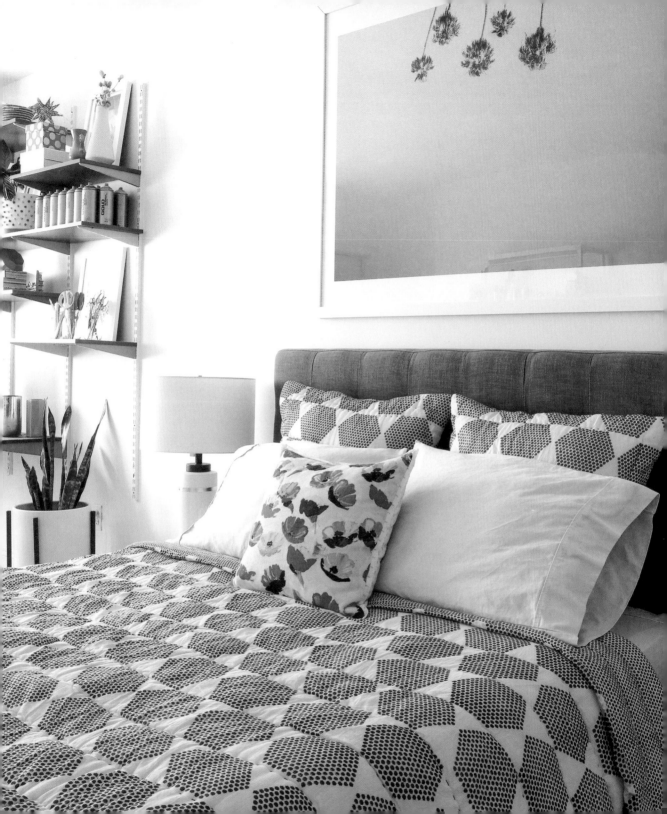

# Chapter Four

---

# THE
# BEDROOM

The place to unplug, unwind, reset. This room is
the first thing you see when you open your eyes each morning,
and it can really create a mood for your entire day. Set yourself
up for happiness and fun with lovely objects to fill your space,
and feel excited and energized when you wake up!

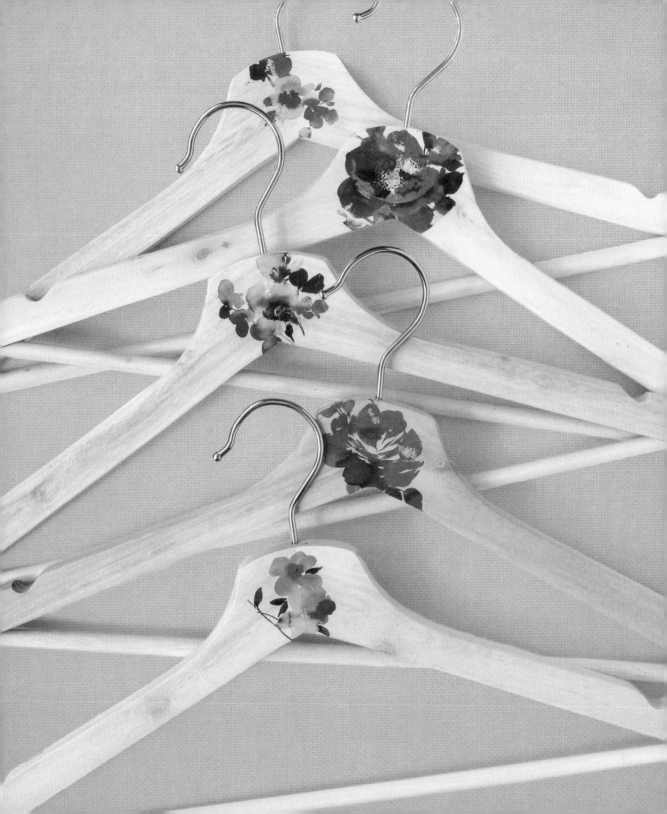

# WOODEN HANGER MAKEOVER

Wooden hangers

Temporary tattoos

Scissors

Sponge

Towel

Mod Podge

Brush

Clothing aside, your closet may not seem like a place for color, but think again! Create gorgeous patterned hangers in minutes without being an artist or even making a mess. The trick? Temporary tattoos! That's right—they're not just for kids (or for skin!). They may seem like a simple detail, but it's one that will make you smile on the days you decide to skip the sweatpants and dress up instead.

*I found wooden hangers at Ikea and temporary tattoos online at Tattly (the designs shown opposite and on page 134 are by Helen Dealtry). You can also make your own by printing with an ink-jet printer on tattoo paper. Try applying the tattoos to other surfaces like vases, ornaments, planters, and more!*

1. If needed, use scissors to trim your tattoo to fit the hanger. Peel the plastic off the front of the design and place it facedown on your hanger, so the white paper back is facing you.

2. Apply pressure with a damp sponge for about 30 seconds. Slowly lift the paper to reveal the tattoo. Lightly dab off excess water with a towel and leave your hanger to air-dry. Repeat with remaining hangers.

3. Seal the designs by brushing on a layer of Mod Podge and let dry. You're all done!

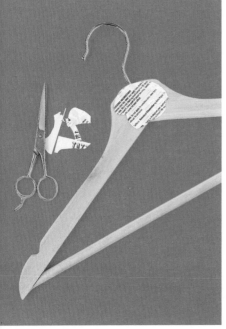

# INSTAGRAM
# WALL ART

4-inch-square photo prints

4-inch-square wooden blocks, about ½" thick

Metal picture hangers, picture hooks with nails and hammer, or removable hook-and-loop strips (optional)

Acrylic paint

Paintbrush

Paper plate or paint palette

Mod Podge

Though my love for Instagram runs deep, one thing I really miss is having physical copies of my photos. If you're like me—sick of having to scroll to find your favorite moments—then it's time to get your memories off your phone and into your home! What better way to display them than by turning them into wall art. This project is amazingly easy and can be done for under thirty bucks!

*If you don't have a printer, some websites will print your photos at a 4-by-4-inch size (see Resources, page 165, for suggestions). If you have no access to a saw to cut your wooden blocks, look online (e.g., Etsy) for pieces already cut. The dimensions can differ from those suggested here; just make sure the photos and wooden blocks are the same size.*

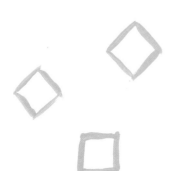

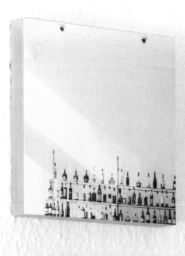
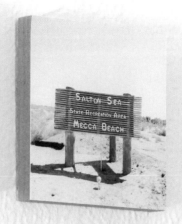
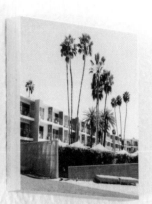
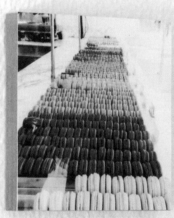
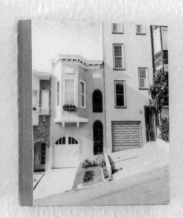
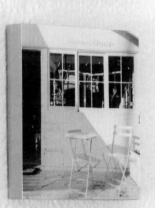
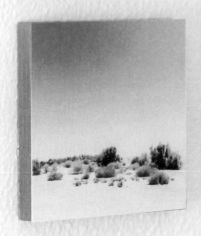
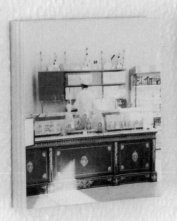
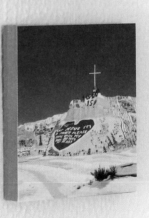

1   If you plan to hang your blocks with nails, then first attach
    hangers to the backs of the blocks using the accompanying
    hardware (usually metal saw-tooth hangers come with small
    nails or screws). However, I recommend using removable hook-
    and-loop strips. They won't hurt walls, which is great if you're
    renting, and the art will hang flat. Or skip the hanging stage
    altogether! If the block is at least $\frac{1}{2}$ inch thick, it will stand
    perfectly on its own.

2   Paint the edges of the wooden blocks. Don't worry if you get
    paint on the front and back since the back will face the wall and
    the photo will cover the front. Let dry.

3   Affix the photo to the block: Make sure your hands are clean so
    that you don't get fingerprints or smudges on your photo, then
    apply a thin layer of Mod Podge to the block and carefully place
    your photo on top. When the photo is in the desired position, lay
    the block flat to dry.

4   Using the picture hooks or hook-and-loop strips, hang the
    blocks on your wall in a grid, geometric or freeform shape, or
    any way you like. Sit back and admire!

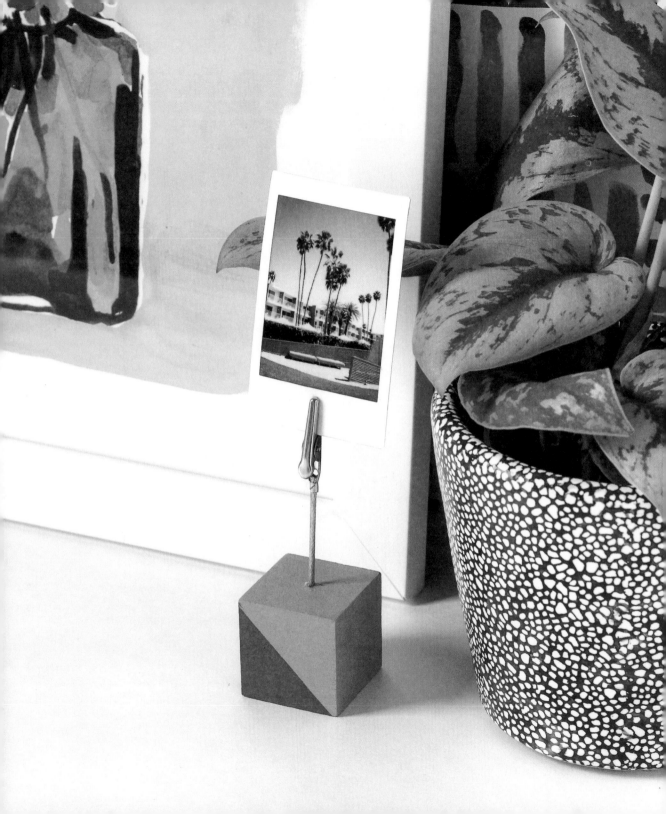

# MINI PHOTO BLOCKS

## MATERIALS

Wooden blocks

Ruler

Drill and drill bit ($^7/_{64}$ size)

Sandpaper

Painter's tape

Paint and paintbrush

Paper plate or paint palette

Alligator clips with wire

E-6000 glue

We all have photos lying around that just don't fit traditional frames: the Polaroids, the wallet-size school portraits, the printed pics that are smaller because you've cut out an ex, etc. Instead of tucking those memories into a drawer, make these easy photo blocks! Unlike a frame with backing and glass, the clip allows you to swap photos within seconds so you can change things up more often. Plus, it takes only about thirty minutes to whip up a set, so there's really no reason not to give this one a try!

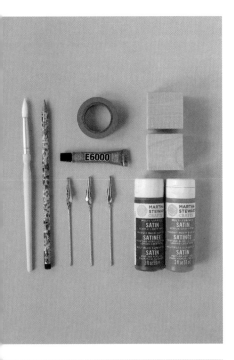

1. Drill a hole in the center of your wooden block for the alligator clip. First, use a ruler to find the center and mark it with a pencil. You want to drill down as far as possible without going through the block. (Though even if you do, the project will still work. You'll just have to be a bit careful when gluing the clip.) If you're new to using a drill, measure the height of your block, then just tape your drill bit at a height just shorter than your block's so you know where to stop. This will also help keep your photo height consistent if you plan on making a set of blocks.

2. Sand any rough spots that were created by drilling so that your block is smooth.

3. Paint as you please! Use the tape to create a color block pattern, or paint a heart, dots, or even your initials.

4. Once the paint is dry, apply a bit of E-6000 glue to the end of your alligator clip and insert it into your block. If you use too much glue, wipe the excess with a damp cloth right away. Allow glue to dry completely.

5. Add your favorite pictures! These photo blocks are perfect for decorating your office wall or a shelf in your home, and they make great gifts (especially if displaying a cute picture of you).

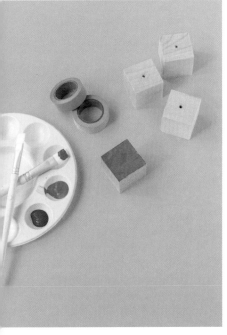

# COLORFUL MIRROR

MATERIALS

Metal picture hanger, picture hook and nail, and hammer for wall mounting (optional)

Square piece of wood

Ruler or measuring tape

Pencil

Painter's tape

Paint and paintbrush

Paper plate or paint palette

Clear shellac

Round mirror

E-6000 glue

It's amazing how often we use a mirror: taking a last-minute look before leaving the house, swiping off makeup at the end of the day, or even just snapping a selfie when we're feeling extra good. With this simple project, your mirror will pop with color and double as wall art even when your beautiful face isn't reflected within.

*When selecting the wood backing, think about how you'll display your mirror. You can either prop it on a dresser or vanity or hang it on the wall. If hanging, avoid wood that's super heavy. You really only need it for mounting the mirror and adding texture and a bit of color, so it can be thin and lightweight. I bought a precut 2-foot-square sheet of plywood at a big-box store.*

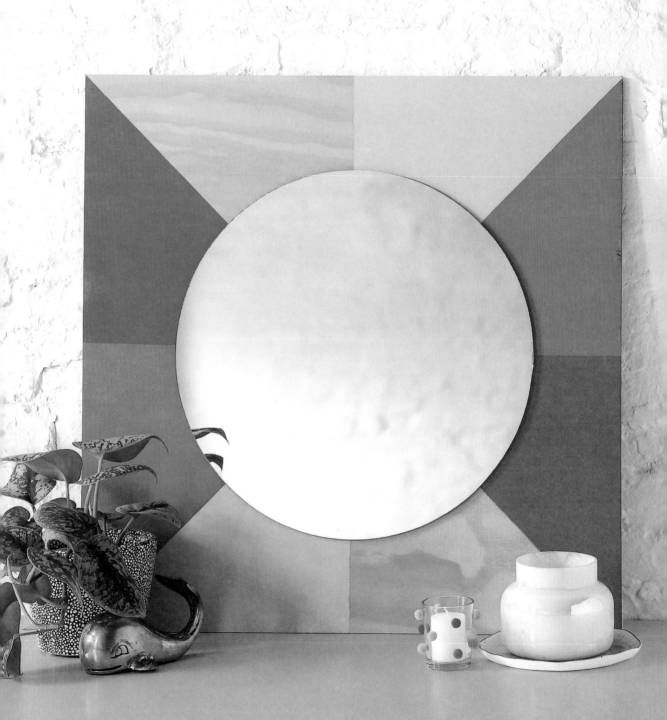

1. If you plan to hang your mirror on a wall, first mount a picture hanger to the wood backing before attaching the mirror, so that you don't break the mirror when hammering on the other side. Use the ruler to find the center of one of the square's edges, then use the hardware included with your picture hanger to attach it an inch or so below the edge.

2. Get to painting! For a multicolor pinwheel design like the one shown, measure and mark a dot in the center of your board. Working on half at a time, lay tape from the center of the dot to the corner of the board, sectioning off for different colors. Apply paint in sections, peeling and reapplying the tape as you work. If you don't want any woodgrain to show, apply a second coat of paint. Don't forget to paint the sides of the wood, too, for that extra pop of color!

3. Seal with a layer of clear shellac and let dry.

4. Attach the mirror: Apply a generous amount of E-6000 glue to the mirror back, staying about half an inch inside the edge so that glue doesn't seep out the sides. Flip the mirror, position it in the center of the square, and carefully affix it to the wood.

5. Lay the mirror flat overnight to dry, then hang it on the wall or prop it in a place that's perfect for reflecting.

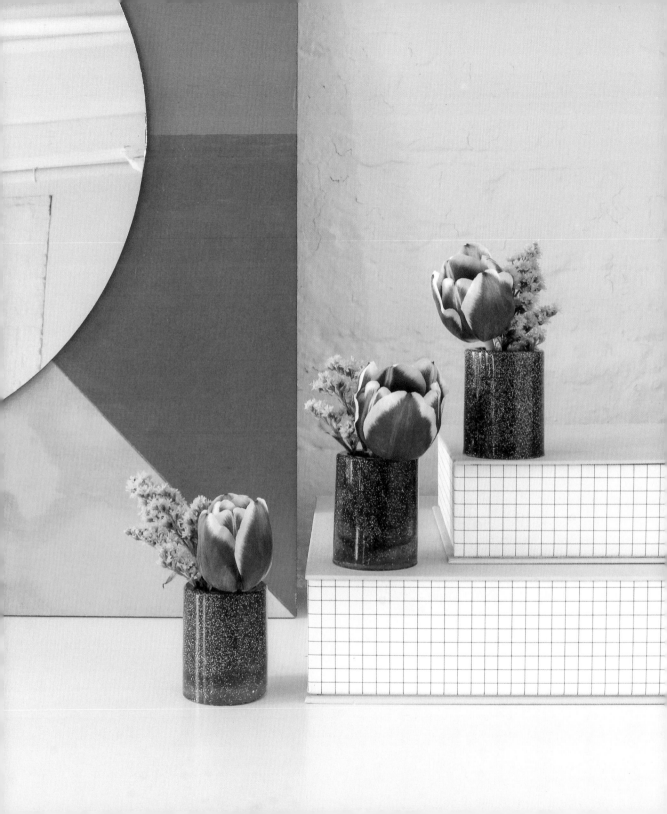

# MINI
# BUD VASE

Cardboard or newspaper

Clear casting epoxy resin

Plastic cups

Popsicle sticks

Silicone dessert cup mold

Glitter

Greens or flowers

The joy of stumbling upon the perfect leaf or branch on a walk around the neighborhood or in your backyard is just like the joy of eating ice cream on a summer's day—only this joy is free! Buying bouquets is great (and I encourage you to treat yourself to one whenever you can); but sometimes all you need is a small pick-me-up, and a simple foraged green will do the trick. What better way to display your find than in a cute vase like this?

*The best part about this project is that you can actually wash the glittery vase and pieces will not flake off. As long as you keep the cap securely on your glitter and don't knock over the bottle, your home should remain glitter free. It's a crafting miracle! Use a mold with a raised center (sometimes sold as a shot glass mold) to create the vase's interior. For a fun tray or centerpiece, affix a few to a ceramic dish using E-6000 glue.*

1   To avoid dripping epoxy on your furniture, cover your work station with cardboard or newspaper, and be sure to set up in a well-ventilated area.

2   In a plastic cup, mix epoxy according to the manufacturer's instructions. Most call for a 1:1 ratio and a double-pour mixture, but it's best to follow instructions. If you're new to working with epoxy, check out my tips on page 34. Just remember: you cannot reuse the mold for food—it's not safe!

3   Pour glitter into the epoxy mixture and stir. The glitter will settle at the bottom of the mold, so you can be generous if you want your piece to be sparkly throughout.

4   Pour the epoxy mixture into the silicone mold and let it harden overnight.

5   Pop the piece out of your mold, fill with greens, and enjoy!

# POM-POM VOTIVE
# CANDLE HOLDER

Glass votive candle holders

Mini pom-poms

Hot-glue gun

Tea light candles

There's no doubt about it—pom-poms make just about anything more adorable. These cute dots of color can embellish most, if not all, surfaces. What's even better is that the mini versions come pre-made, which means your crafting time for this project is instantly cut in half! In five minutes or less you can put together these whimsical candle holders. Make one to keep on your dresser, or create a dozen and use as a centerpiece. I have a feeling that once you start gluing, it'll be hard to stop. Plus this project is so easy, it's nearly impossible to mess up!

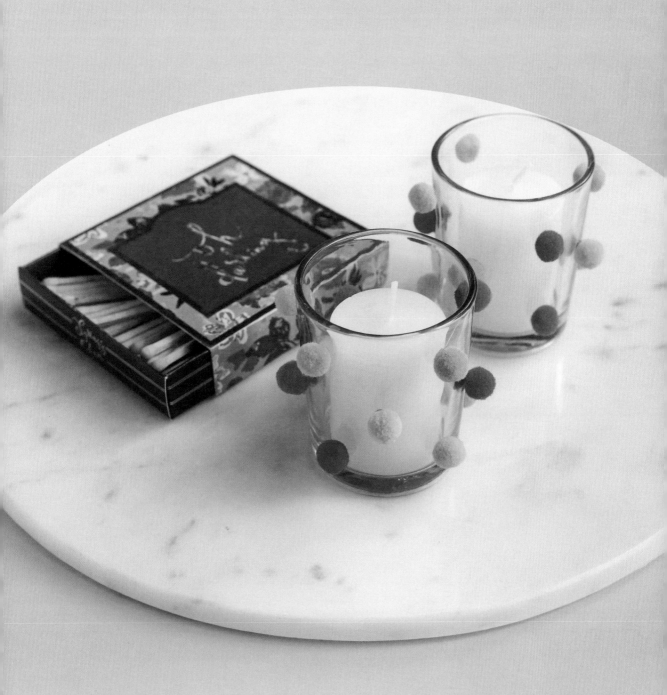

1   Dab glue onto the back of your pom-pom and position it on the
    votive. You'll want to work about $\frac{1}{2}$ inch or more from the top
    of the candle to avoid contact with flames. You really don't need
    much glue, since you want to avoid excess peeking out the side
    of your pom.

2   Repeat, repeat, repeat until your votive is covered to your
    liking. Pop in some tea light candles and enjoy the glow!

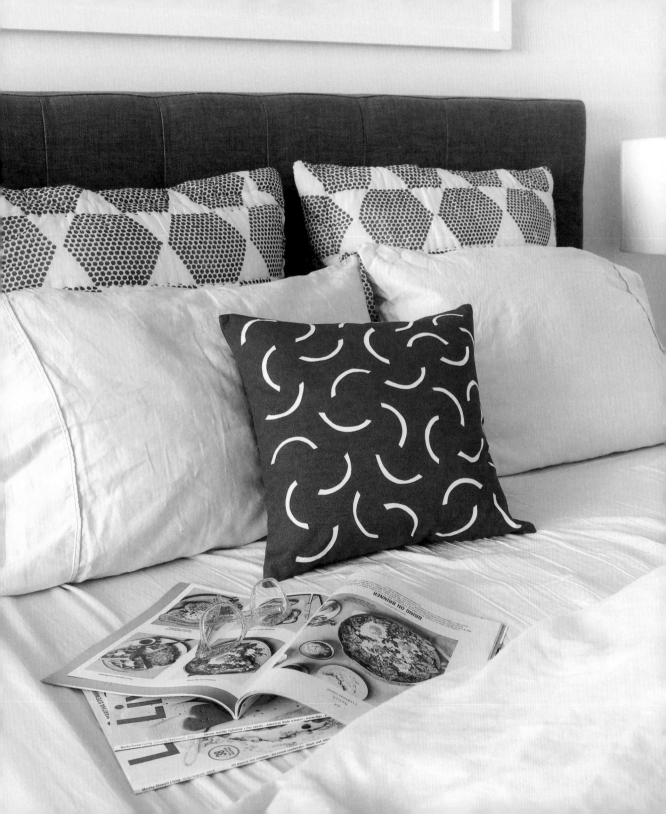

# GEOMETRIC PATTERNED PILLOW

MATERIALS

Iron-on vinyl

Pillowcase and pillow

Pencil

Scissors

Iron and ironing board

If you haven't crafted with iron-transfer vinyl, then get ready for a new addiction! This type of heat transfer is great because there's no paint cleanup or mess. Plus, whatever design you create will be exactly how your project turns out. No surprises, just perfection—and done in a matter of minutes! Really, this material is the stuff dreams are made of.

*This technique isn't just for pillows. Get ready to iron vinyl onto everything in your home! Best of all, you don't need a cutting machine (like a Silhouette or Cricut) to use the iron-on vinyl rolls sold at large craft stores. They certainly help create more intricate shapes and patterns, but you can easily cut your own. Vinyl is not cheap, though, so before you get scissor happy, try your design with scrap paper first.*

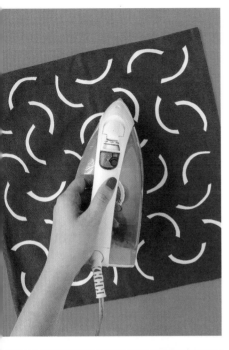

1. If you're nervous about cutting your design freehand, sketch it first on the back of the vinyl. Keep in mind that your image will be reversed when you iron it on, so be sure to draw letters or numbers backward to read correctly when flipped.

2. Cut out your design: Place the matte side of the vinyl facedown, with the shiny side facing you. Use the scissors to cut around your sketch.

3. Iron your pillowcase to smooth out wrinkles. Arrange the vinyl pieces on the pillowcase.

4. Set the iron to temperature according to the manufacturer's instruction. Press the iron over the vinyl pieces, holding it in each spot for about 45 seconds to one minute. Move the iron until the entire design has been covered. Flip the pillowcase inside out and repeat for the back of the design.

5. Turn the pillowcase right side out, remove the protective cover from the vinyl, insert your pillow, and take a nap!

# MINI BOOKCASE MAKEOVER

## MATERIALS

Small square white laminate bookcase

Newspaper or drop cloth

Paint

Paintbrush and palette

Paint roller

Painter's tape (optional)

Acrylic crystal-clear top coat

Blanket

Screw-in legs (6" tall)

Top plates and screws for legs

Pencil

Power drill and drill bit in the size of your screws

Screwdriver

For months I searched for a cute record player stand that was in my budget, but somehow I kept coming up short. Instead of spending more time scouring the internet, or giving in to the temptation to break my bank account, I decided to give a cheaper bookcase a makeover. With a bit of paint and an added boost of height, this colorful $30 unit became an instant favorite in my home.

*I used a Kallax unit from Ikea, but you could find similar models at any big-box or discount department store. I found the legs online for less than $4 apiece, but they're widely available in retail stores, too. If you'd rather not paint the legs, or if you're looking for a fun and unique shape, Pretty Pegs (prettypegs.com) sells amazing ones specifically for Ikea furniture.*

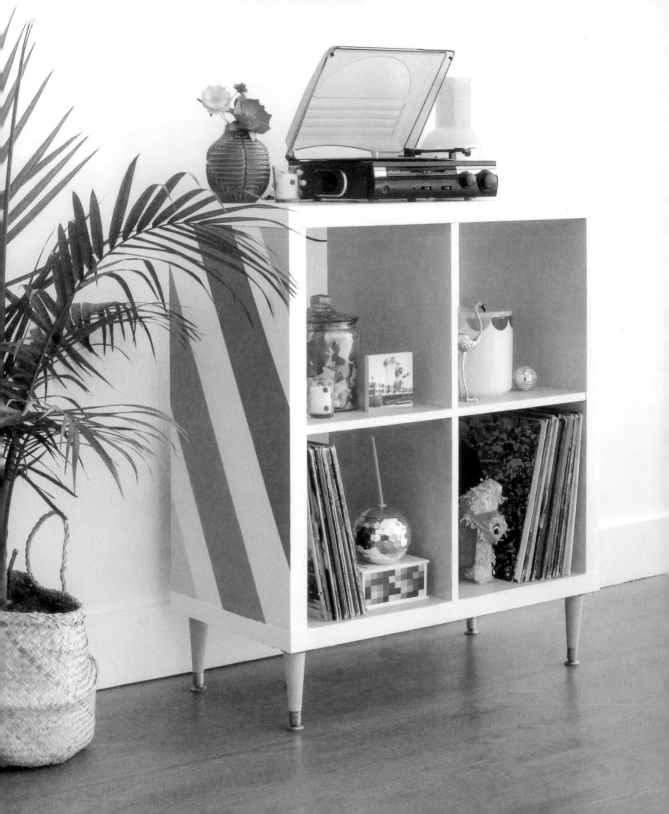

1. Lay out your newspaper or drop cloth. If you decide to paint the legs, start there! Use the paintbrush to cover them in a pretty color and set aside so that while they're drying, you can assemble the bookcase.

2. If your bookcase came as a flat-pack, assemble it on the drop cloth according to the directions.

3. After everything is assembled, it's time to paint! You can go to town and paint the entire unit, but for a subtler approach, use the roller to paint just the inside of the cubbies, leaving you with pop of color that will peek out from behind your items. The roller will not only help you finish faster but also eliminate brushstrokes. Let dry.

4. Add detail to the sides if you'd like: If you painted the outside of the bookcase as well as the interior, make sure it's completely dry before taping off a design (such as a geometric pattern) and filling in with a different color of paint. You may have to apply more than one coat. Because the surface of the unit is finished, peel off the tape as soon as you finish, and before the paint is dry, so the paint does not peel up with it, too. (Even if you're using an unfinished bookcase, it still doesn't hurt to peel up right away.) You can spot-clean any mistakes with a damp cloth at this time, too.

5. Once your bookcase is dry, move it to a well-ventilated area and spray the painted portions with clear top coat; let dry.

6. Drill the leg holes: Lay out your blanket (to avoid scratching or damaging the top of the bookcase) and flip the bookcase upside down. Align the top plates in the corners and mark the hole positions with a pencil. Remove the top plates and drill your holes

with a bit that's the same size as your screw. You'll only need to drill in as deep as your screw is long. Replace the top plate and secure in place with a screw.

7 Screw the legs tightly into the top plates and turn the bookcase right side up. You now have a fun new display stand! Use it to hold your favorite records, books, or any other household knick-knacks you choose. You can even swap out the legs for wheels, add a handle to the top, and turn it into a bar cart!

# Staging a Beautiful Bookcase

Oh, the bookcase, aka the storage locker for all those expensive college textbooks you can't bear to part with. If you're looking to style your shelving to show off a more polished look (as well as how smart you are), then follow these few basic tips.

**HIDE CLUTTER.** Let's be real: our homes are not magazine-worthy at all times. We all own items that, though they maybe functional or sentimental, are not pretty to look at. In other words, we all have a bit of clutter. But you can make that clutter look good with some closed storage. Boxes on open shelving will hide mismatched items while still looking uniform. They're also a great way to add some weight to your shelf.

**ADD BOOKS.** Stack them both horizontally and vertically for a bit of variety, or group by size. Try playing with color, maybe stacking books of the same color together or creating mini-rainbows. If your bookcase is not especially tall or narrow, it helps to divide the shelves into thirds, creating balance with three separate vignettes.

**ADD DECORATIVE OBJECTS.** Not every shelf needs books. Vases and bottles are great for filling the space and bringing in new shapes; pick round vessels to contrast with the straight lines of the books and frames. Layer the bigger vases together, then place smaller, shorter objects in front. This is a great way to weave in those special keepsakes and vintage finds that make your shelving unique.

**ADD ART.** Framed artwork adds height and can make your shelf seem fuller, plus it's a simple way to bring in extra color. Cute photos of you, your friends, or your travels work, too! (Check out the Mini Photo Blocks on page 135.)

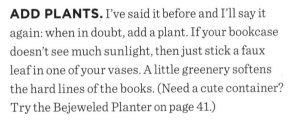

**ADD PLANTS.** I've said it before and I'll say it again: when in doubt, add a plant. If your bookcase doesn't see much sunlight, then just stick a faux leaf in one of your vases. A little greenery softens the hard lines of the books. (Need a cute container? Try the Bejeweled Planter on page 41.)

You can stick to books, and books only, but even if you don't want a bookcase that's too decorative, just layer smaller pieces like photographs or trinkets in the corners for a mini vignette.

No matter what objects you're working with, mix heights to make your styling aesthetically pleasing. Variety will create balance and help your eyes flow from one section to another. When you're styling, it's important to move items into a few

configurations before settling on one. Since people rarely look at your bookcase close up, get some perspective by stepping back to see how each vignette looks. You won't style everything perfectly the first time—in fact, you may need fifteen attempts before the space starts to come together. Or you may find that you need to DIY or buy a few more items to fill the shelves, but don't let that dissuade you because you can totally pull this off. Turn on some music, pour a little wine from your stylish bar cart (see page 55), and have fun. If worse comes to worse (which I don't think it will), you can always sell all your books—well, all except this one, that is!

# Pastels

If you're looking to transition away from what I like to call "apartment beige" but aren't quite ready to go over-the-top bold, pastels are a nice, subtle way to add color to your entire home. Unlike other colors that start with a base and then add a small amount of white or black to be lighter or darker, pastels start with a white/cream base and add only a small amount of color to it, making these colors much paler. They're desaturated without being completely white, making them the perfect solution if you want just a hint of a hue.

Even though pastels tend to read as soft—and they're not as intimidating as bold or bright colors—it's completely understandable to be hesitant about them. If you get the wrong shade, your home could end up looking like an oversized nursery. But like I said, I'm your color tour guide and I would never put you in that situation! To keep your home sophisticated and oh so adult, here are some go-to choices that are sure to give you great results.

**MILLENNIAL PINK:**
Certainly the "it" color of (apparently) an entire generation, but to me it's still a color classic. This soft rosy hue can be paired with a warm gray or white for a light and airy look, or with black and gold for a more dramatic effect.

**POWDER BLUE:**
Pair this cool tint with richer colors like navy and red to avoid making rooms look like a baby nursery.

**MINT:**
Fresh and classic! For a monochromatic look, try painting mint alongside hunter green and gold. Mint also looks great with whites.

**PEACH:**
A major step up from traditional beige—it has much more warmth and brightness. Contrast this color with rich brown furniture or floors.

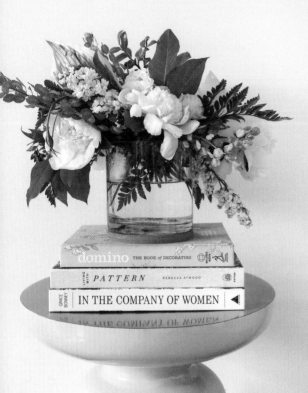

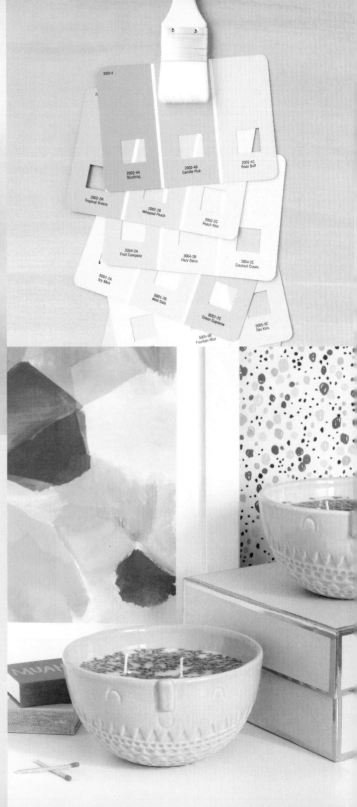

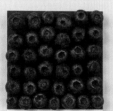

**PANTONE** 19-3935
Deep Cobalt

## HOW TO APPLY

Instead of using lots of pastels together (and making your home feel like an Easter basket), add them as soft accents instead. When in doubt, stick with one. You'll also want to avoid pairing pastels with bold colors in equal proportion. Because the hues of the colors have different vibrancies, they will clash more than complement if used in the same amount in a given space. Pastels tend to look best when they're complementing a richer color either as an accent or dominating as the only color in a white space. They're a bit tricky to work with, but when done right, they can make a room come across much softer and inviting.

If you're consider updating your interior paint with pastels, start by covering just a wall or two. It's important to test the color on the wall before committing: because the color is so subtle, it can read dramatically different depending on the light. However, the nice thing is that you can paint over a pastel paint job more easily than most other colors, so don't be afraid to have a little fun. And if you really, really can't paint your walls, trying putting up an oversized wall hanging in a lovely pastel shade.

### GIVE IT SOME DEPTH

*Pastels don't have to be flat. If you're ready to experiment with wallpaper, pastel patterns are a great choice since their softness keeps them from being overwhelming. Everything from geometrics to light textured patterns looks lovely in pastels, but floral designs are a particularly natural fit for lighter tints.*

## GET RESTFUL AND RELAXED

*Soothing pastels in the bedroom can help you unwind at the end of the day. But don't limit yourself just to wall colors and textiles—even your wall art can bring in a nice soft pastel shade (like that beautiful sky behind the palm trees!). A bold accent accessory will keep the room looking grounded and mature.*

## LIGHTEN UP YOUR FURNITURE

*Furniture might not be the first thing to come to mind when considering where to add pastels, but I absolutely recommend it. This mint green softens the more industrial texture of the wall and picks up some of the leafy color of the plant—win win! If you're painting furniture yourself, opt for white or light-colored pieces (or prime them first) to keep the pastel nice and soft.*

# Photography Tips

Now that your home is freshly decorated and full of dozens of beautiful handmade accents, it's time to share it with the world! Or, at the very least, with friends, family, and all those old high school friends on Facebook. (Because after all that crafting, you've earned the right to make them a little jealous, yeah?) To make your hard work really shine, and to claim supreme bragging rights, take some photos to share. This task might be stressful, but you don't have to be a professional shutterbug to take a beautiful photo. All you need is to follow a few simple tips.

## EQUIPMENT

There's no need to shell out for a new camera—cameras on smartphones are incredibly sophisticated and work just fine for most shoots. Instead of taking the photos in specific apps like Instagram and posting immediately, use the default camera app. Shooting in the camera app allows you to take many more photos, giving you plenty of variations to choose from. Just make sure the lens is free of smudges (use a glasses-cleaning cloth or screen wipe to clear it) and not covered or blocked by a phone case.

But if a phone just isn't cutting it, upgrade to a point-and-shoot digital camera. Most models give great picture quality without sacrificing the pocket size of a smartphone, and they're available for a few hundred dollars. Don't get too hung up on megapixels; what's more important is sensor size, autofocus, and image stabilization. Look for models with a CMOS sensor (instead of an older CCD), especially for shooting in low-lit conditions.

If you want to take your photos one step further (or even have your photos published either online or in a magazine), it may be worth investing in a DSLR camera. These professional-level cameras will cost a good deal more than a point-and-shoot (especially because you buy lenses separately!), but in return they give you more control over shutter speed, ISO (the higher the max ISO, the more sensitive the camera is to light), and file type. You can rent a nice camera and a lens for the shoot if you're not looking to make the investment, scour the internet for discounted prices on the previous year's models, or even hit up eBay.

Regardless of what you shoot with, I recommend the following tools for the best pictures possible:

+ **TRIPOD** (to avoid blurriness)

+ **WIRELESS REMOTE** (for DSLR and some point-and-shoot cameras)

+ **REFLECTOR** (more on this below)

+ **WINE**

(Okay, so mayyybe you don't need the wine, but it certainly wouldn't hurt.)

## STAGING

Because the camera captures exactly what's in front of it, it's important to stage your photograph. Don't be fooled—even the most "casual" shots you've seen online have been carefully curated. Just because things lie around your house in real life doesn't mean they have to be so in the photo. Ugly remote collection? Stash it before shooting! A thousand chewed-up dog toys? Set them aside! Just as you don't want to take a selfie in a mirror when the background is a disaster—people will fixate on the mess, not you—you want all the focus to be on your home and don't want viewers to get sidetracked by knickknacks or clutter.

## LIGHTING

When shooting, try to use natural light as much as possible. Turn off overhead lighting to avoid yellowish tints, and use sunlight from a bright window for a nice even color. If your shoot day is flexible, keep track of what the lighting is like in your space for a day or two. Note the times it's the brightest and take some test shots to compare the results.

While natural light is a must, it can also get harsh if it's hitting your subject directly. The photo on the top was taken close to a window with no curtain. The photo on the bottom was taken with a translucent screen (you can use a sheer curtain) over the window.

Additionally, I used a reflector to bounce light back on the left side of the bottom photo. Reflectors do just what their name suggests— reflect light to soften shadows. You can pick up expensive reflectors at photography stores,

but they're easy to create at home: angle either a reflector or piece of white poster board to catch the light from a window and reflect it onto the surface you're photographing.

When you pair these techniques, everything becomes less harsh and your home seems much more soft and inviting—just like you see it in real life!

## USING YOUR TRIPOD

So you know all those photos you've pinned, re-grammed, and drooled over? The ones that made you hate your apartment and made you want to move because they're so bright and perfect? More often than not, a tripod is to thank for that magic. Trust me: a tripod will change everything, because it gives you the freedom to use a slower shutter speed on a DSLR, allowing more light in and making spaces appear brighter than they are, or to avoid blurs or shakiness when shooting on a phone or compact camera. Photo shoots with a tripod will take longer because you have to set up and frame each shot instead of moving freely while holding the camera, but your photos will display a brightness you wouldn't otherwise achieve.

Another way to avoid blur in your photos is to use a wireless remote: the less you touch the camera on the tripod, the better. Plus, a remote will allow you to move around the room to do other things like bounce or diffuse light.

DSLR tripods are available online and in camera shops, but you can also find inexpensive mini-tripods for smartphones that provide much of the same blur-fighting benefits. No tripod? Brace your elbow against your body to steady your phone as you snap a quick picture.

## COMPOSITION

When it comes to finding the best composition, move around and shoot from as many perspectives as possible. A full-room shot, a detail shot, partially cropped—get it all! In a properly styled photo, no fancy angles are needed because the space should speak for itself: if you find you're lying on the floor and pointing the camera in a weird direction, you're doing it wrong. Shoot straight-on to start. To get a variant look, change the height or distance, not the angle, of the camera from the object.

Taking a variety of full-room and detail shots will give the viewer the sense they've been in your space and know what everything looks like. Don't be afraid to move items around while shooting until you find the right balance—sometimes all it takes to get the perfect composition is to nudge something a few inches to the left. And since the camera will capture the scene differently than your eye will, check through your shots as you work to make sure they're turning out as you'd like. Is one item closer to another, creating a strange gap? Are all the items on one side of the setup, making it feel heavy? Take the time to critique, adjust, and readjust before shooting: it's significantly easier to get the image you want in the moment than to crop at the editing stage, and it's better to adjust midshoot than to start editing, hate the way something looks, and have to reshoot.

## EDITING

You don't need to spend hours and hours on editing, but a few simple tweaks can really enhance your photos. For software, I recommend Adobe Lightroom on the computer; for the phone, VSCO and Snapseed are my go-to apps. There are *tons* of options, so download a few different apps, test out the tools, and see which ones you like best.

Although individual aesthetics vary, these are the features that will generally need tweaking on every photo:

+ **EXPOSURE:** brightens the image

+ **CONTRAST:** helps brighten and make colors pop

+ **SHARPEN:** makes your photos as crisp as possible, adding a little *oomph*

+ **VIBRANCE:** amps up the color

Of course, we all want every detail of our homes to be picture-perfect at all times, but let's be real, when is it ever? If you notice a small imperfection after you shoot (let's say a piece of dust under the couch), it's totally fine to remove it in Photoshop. If you're on a smartphone, the TouchRetouch app is perfect for small corrections.

And that's it! You did it! You made all the projects (well, hopefully at least one), you styled and photographed your home, you drank all the wine. All that's left to do now is sit back, hit Publish, and watch the comments roll in!

P.S. I totally want to see your space! If sharing on social media, please tag me at @thecraftedlife so I can be jealous too!

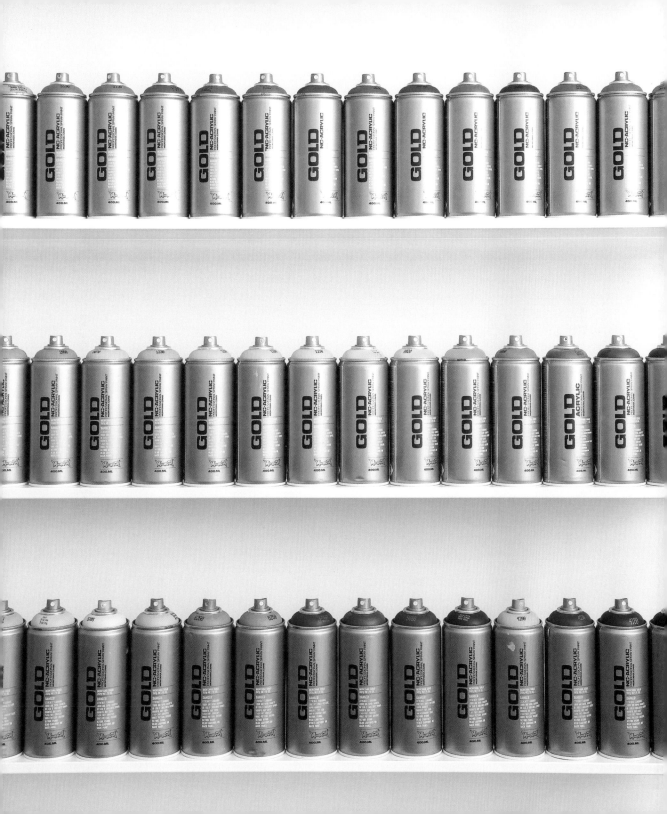

# Resources

## HOME DECOR

### West Elm
www.WestElm.com
*Modern furniture, home decor, and home accessories*

### CB2
www.CB2.com
*Modern furniture and home decor*

### Crate and Barrel
www.CrateandBarrel.com
*Stylish furniture, kitchenware, and home essentials*

### H&M Home
www.hm.com/department/home
*Interior design and decoration*

### ABC Carpet and Home
www.ABChome.com
*Furniture, home decor, and carpeting*

### Terrain
www.ShopTerrain.com
*Home and garden decor, furniture, found objects, and antiques*

### Anthropologie
www.anthropologie.com
*Furniture, home decor, accessories, and more*

### Lulu & Georgia
www.LuluandGeorgia.com
*Rugs, furniture, pillows, throws, and more*

### AllModern
www.AllModern.com
*Furniture, lighting, accents, and decor*

### Wayfair
www.wayfair.com
*Furniture, lighting, and cookware*

### Target
www.target.com
*Furniture, patio and garden, kitchenware, and accessories*

### Blu Dot
www.BluDot.com
*Contemporary furniture designs and home and office decor*

### Rejuvenation
www.rejuvenation.com
*Period-authentic lighting and hardware*

### Schoolhouse Electric
www.schoolhouse.com
*Period and modern lighting, furniture, and hardware*

## PHOTO PRINTING/ART WORK

### Parabo
www.parabo.press
*Photo prints, books, cards, and display supplies*

### Artifact Uprising
www.ArtifactUprising.com
*Custom photo books, cards, prints, and frames*

### Artfully Walls
www.ArtfullyWalls.com
*Art prints and curated gallery walls*

### Minted
www.minted.com
*Art, apparel, and home goods from independent artists*

### Society 6
www.society6.com
*Art, apparel, and home goods from independent artists*

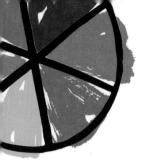

## CREATE YOUR OWN
# Color Palette

**ONE**

**TWO**

**THREE**

**FOUR**

**FIVE**

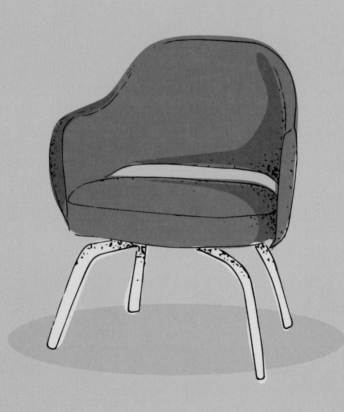

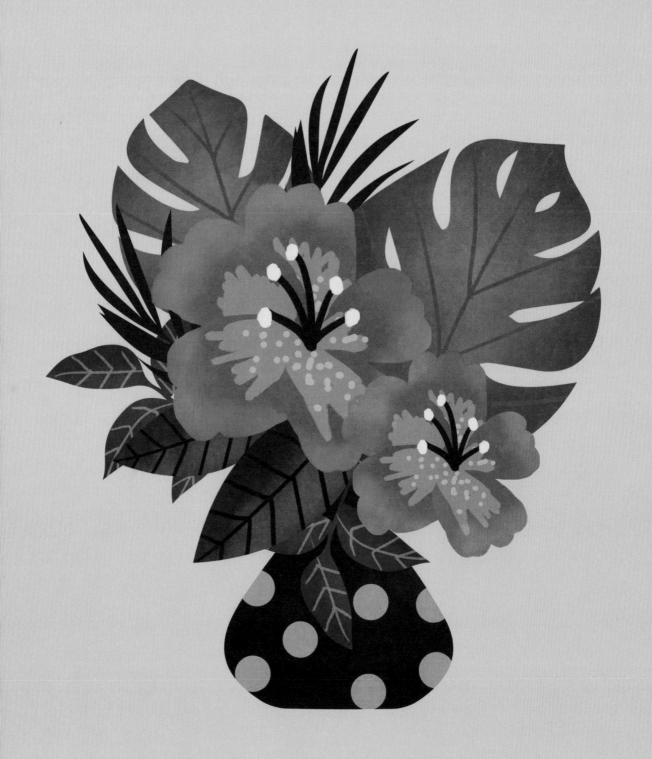

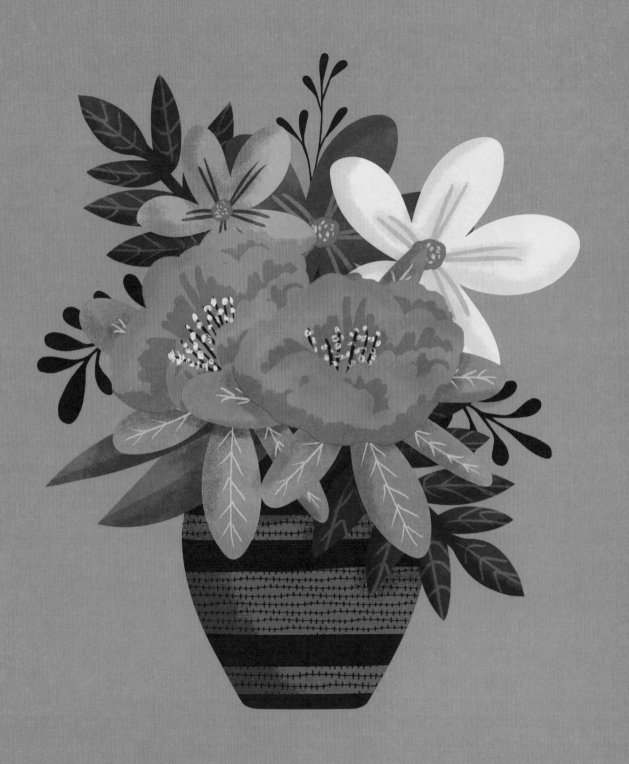

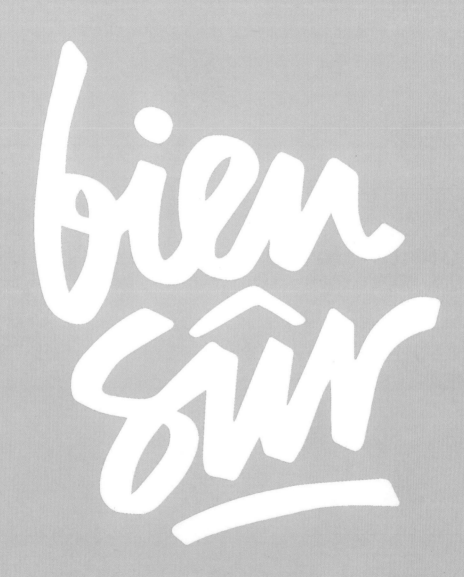

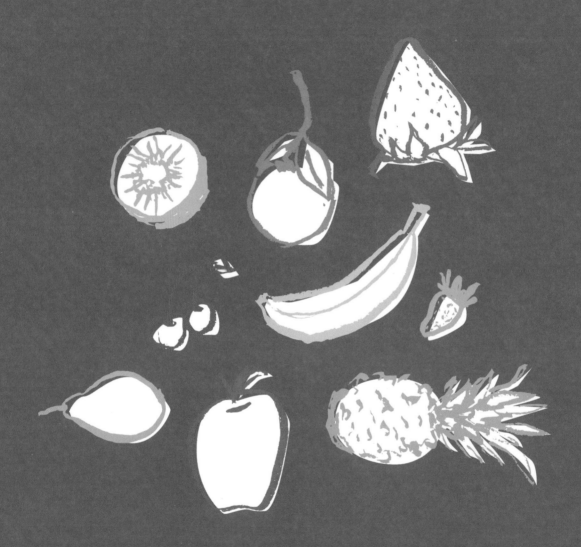

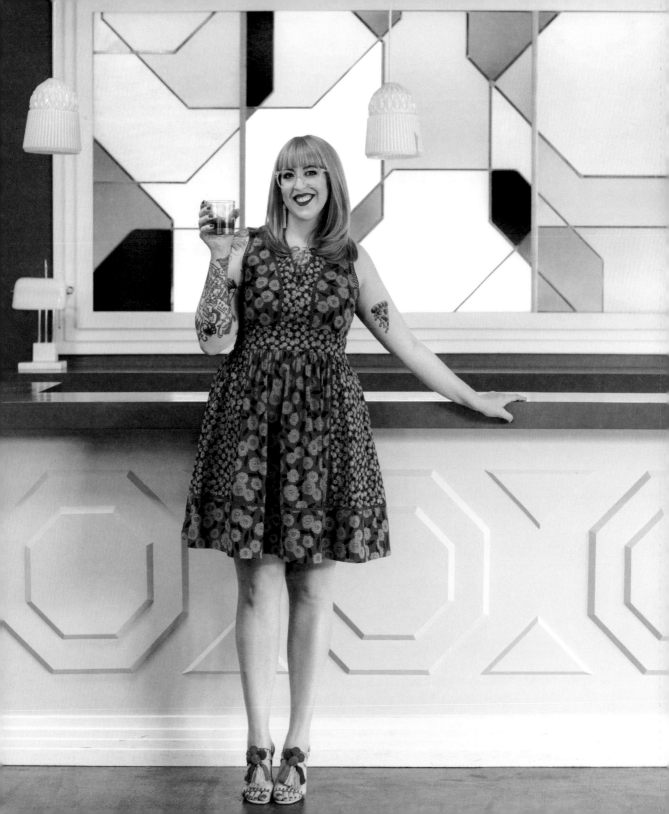

# About the Author

Rachel Mae Smith is a lifestyle writer, photographer, and author of the popular blog *The Crafted Life*. Her work centers on making fun and colorful projects using accessible items and techniques to help readers create items that convey personal style without stress. She has been featured in *Martha Stewart Living*, *Better Homes & Gardens*, and *Real Simple*, among others. When she's not brushing glitter out of her hair, you can find her exploring and color hunting around the world. Visit her online at www.thecraftedlife.com and on Instagram at @thecraftedlife.

# Acknowledgments

This book would not exist without the wonderful and generous people I've met along the way. They include my agent, Lilly Ghahremani, who has been my biggest champion throughout this project. Blair Thornburgh, Andie Reid, and the rest of the Quirk team for believing in my vision and helping me make it a reality. Ron and Kelly Smith, who never cease to be the best support system anyone can ask for. Sarah Khandjian, Sharon Taylor, Conrad Benner, Carrie Maguire, Julie O'Boyle-Sharp, Abra Boyd, and all of my friends whose love and encouragement got me through those countless 16-hour work days. And Ryan Michaud for always being on my team.

Thank you all for everything.

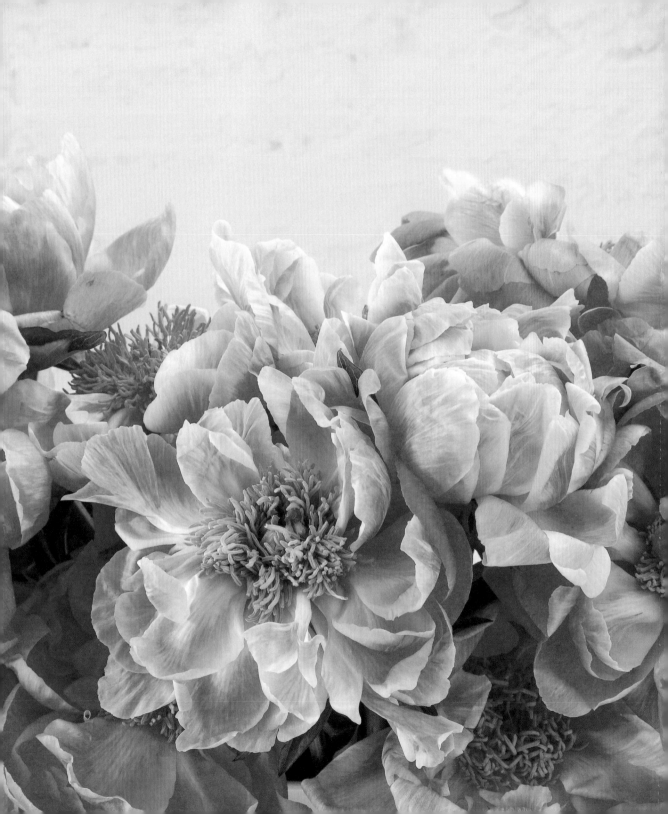